Access your online resources

SEND Intervention is accompanied by a number of printable ~~materials~~, designed to ensure this resource best supports your professional needs.

Activate your online resources:

Go to www.routledge.com/cw/speechmark and click on the cover of this book.

Click the 'Sign in or Request Access' button and follow the instructions in order to access the resources.

Please also visit the Willow Tree Learning website at www.willowtreelearning. co.uk for further resources and examples.

SEND Intervention

The second in *The Essential SENCO Toolkit* series, this resource clarifies and explores the key distinctions between quality first teaching adjustments, resources/support and interventions. It allows practitioners to develop their practice effectively and strategically to capture the true impact of SEND provision, by shifting the focus from the 'who and when' to the 'what and why'.

Chapters also include original frameworks – the 4 Functions of Learning Support – to help with the deployment of teaching assistants and to provide a shared language of support, as well as resources that support the application of the 7 Cs Learning Portfolio (introduced in the first book in the series, *SEND Assessment*) and an intervention index to fully understand the purpose and effectiveness of interventions.

Key features offered:

- An introduction to the 4 Functions of Learning Support, providing a measurable language of learning support to help practitioners to organise and deploy teaching assistants as part of their SEND provision
- An intervention index to enable individual or MAT-based SENCOs to capture their own evidence base regarding the purpose and impact of interventions
- Intervention action cards and targeted outcomes for all 49 themes within the 7 Cs Learning Portfolio
- A photocopiable and downloadable programme of materials that can be used by readers to gain a better understanding of interventions.

SEND Intervention will promote confidence and clarity regarding the rationale for SEND provision. This essential resource provides a practical toolkit to support both new and experienced SENCOs and SEN practitioners.

Judith Carter is a registered Educational Psychologist (EP) and Director of Willow Tree Learning. She is a Tutor on the National Award for SEN Co-ordination working with Eastern Partnership and hosts the Essential SENCO Network and provides a range of bespoke training on SEND. Judith believes passionately in inclusion and education for all and works directly with staff, children, young people and their families, to promote participation and learning.

The Essential SENCO Toolkit Series

The Essential SENCO Toolkit is a series of books containing bespoke resources and frameworks for use by SENCOs and SEN practitioners. Each book contains a range of practical materials, tried-and-tested by members of the Essential SENCO Network. The author, Judith Carter, is an Educational Psychologist with over 20 years' experience. As the Director of Willow Tree Learning and host of the Essential SENCO Network she developed materials to respond directly to the needs expressed by practitioners. This original series provides a starting point to support the development of SEND Assessment, Intervention and Quality Assurance, offering clarity regarding the identification of SEN versus low attainment, and promoting resources to identify those learners with SEN, SEND, learners who are Disabled and those with Medical Needs. This series is essential reading and will aid practice development and offer support and encouragement to all who work in the profession.

Recent titles in the series include:

SEND Assessment
A Strengths-Based Framework for Learners with SEND
Judith Carter

SEND Intervention
Planning Provision with Purpose
Judith Carter

For a complete list of titles in this series, please visit https://www.routledge.com/The-Essential-SENCO-Toolkit

SEND Intervention

Planning Provision with Purpose

JUDITH CARTER

Routledge
Taylor & Francis Group

LONDON AND NEW YORK

Cover design: J Griffin

First published 2022
by Routledge
2 Park Square, Milton Park, Abingdon, Oxon OX14 4RN

and by Routledge
605 Third Avenue, New York, NY 10158

Routledge is an imprint of the Taylor & Francis Group, an informa business

British Library Cataloguing-in-Publication Data
A catalogue record for this book is available from the British Library

Library of Congress Cataloging-in-Publication Data
Names: Carter, Judith, author.
Title: SEND intervention : planning provision with purpose / Judith Carter.
Description: Abingdon, Oxon ; New York : Routledge, 2022. |
Series: The essential SENCO toolkit | Includes bibliographical references and index.
Identifiers: LCCN 2021034228 | ISBN 9781032016481 (hardback) |
ISBN 9781032016474 (paperback) | ISBN 9781003179436 (ebook)
Subjects: LCSH: Learning disabled children—Education. | Effective
teaching. | Special education—Evaluation.
Classification: LCC LC4704 .C376 2021 | DDC 371.9—dc23
LC record available at https://lccn.loc.gov/2021034228

ISBN: 978-1-032-01648-1 (hbk)
ISBN: 978-1-032-01647-4 (pbk)
ISBN: 978-1-003-17943-6 (ebk)

DOI: 10.4324/9781003179436

Typeset in Bembo
by codeMantra

Access the companion website: www.routledge.com/cw/speechmark

Contents

Acknowledgements

This book is dedicated to all of us who are working to improve outcomes for children and young people.

In my acknowledgements for book 1, I described writing the book as a "dream come true". In contrast, book 2 has at times felt far more of a nightmare! I really did wake up worrying about it and was haunted by the fear of the 'sequel' never being as good as the original! I would like to thank the teachers, SENCOs, SEN Practitioners and TAs, who through their conversations reminded me of the purpose of this book. You all do an incredible job and my only hope for the book is that the resources and ideas support you in your work with children, young people and families.

I would also like to express my ongoing thanks to my partner Matt Cooper, who never doubted my capacity, even when I did; my parents, Tony and Dot Carter, for their unconditional love and support; and of course, our now fully grown up Yorkie-poo dog, Sunni, for her insistent demands for fresh air and play, which reminded me to breathe!

Introduction

Welcome to *SEND Intervention: Planning Provision with Purpose*. This is the second book in *The Essential SENCO Toolkit* series and although any of the books can be read individually, it does build upon concepts explored in the first book *SEND Assessment: A Strengths-based Framework for Learners with SEND*. Key concepts from book 1 will be revised and interleaved into this text (particularly in Chapter 2), to act as a reminder of what has previously been written or to provide necessary context. This book shares the intent of all the books in this series, of offering a practical 'starting point' to SENCOs and SEN Practitioners, so it contains resources, frameworks and tools for adaptation and application. In effect, the book has been written to support *you* in your role and to encourage confident reflection regarding the actions you take to support children and young people, particularly those with SEND. It is of course underpinned by theory, which will be referred to, but this is not a theoretical text. As and when time allows, you may choose to use the references provided to strengthen your knowledge and critically consider the theoretical underpinnings of an approach, but the content here is predominantly practical in nature.

As the title suggests, the focus of this book is on SEND intervention. Together, we will explore types of provision offered to learners with SEND, including the distinction between teacher **adjustments**, **support** and **intervention** and consider how these can be planned, deployed and monitored. The focus will be upon SEND provision for all learners with SEND, but on this occasion an explicit distinction will not be made between those learners with an Education, Health and Care Plan (EHCP) or those at SEN Support, unless specifically stated. The rationale for this is that SEND provision relates to all learners and the themes to be explored relate to all learners regardless of SEND status. Of course, you will need to consider the relevance and application of ideas for your individual learners, but you will do so, by thinking of them as individuals rather than whether they have an EHCP or receive SEN support. In real terms, throughout this book, we will consider **what** you do, **why** you do this (and not something else) and **how** you know it makes a difference.

I feel incredibly privileged to have this opportunity of 'working' with you within this context and I assure you that I will do my best to ensure that the time you spend reading this book (as with the others in this series), is an investment of time which will contribute practical ideas, support and options for application. Please feel free to 'scan' the text and select the sections that feel the most relevant to you at this time, or of course, read the whole text and reflect on the key 'starting points' that resonate for you in your setting. If you have read book 1, you will know that I have worked in education for over 25 years, as a Teacher, Educational Psychologist, LA Senior Adviser for SEND and Inclusion, Ofsted Inspector, SEND Consultant and Tutor on the National Award for SEN Co-ordination. Within all of these roles, I have been and continue to be, inspired by the children and families I have met and the educationalists who work with them. They have influenced the ideas presented in this book and many have taken the 'starting point' offered and developed it into a useful and relevant approach in their setting. I hope this will also be the case for you. As you read and reflect, allow your own ideas for possible adaptation and application to emerge and develop and then 'trust' yourself to have a go! If you would like to share your experiences, ideas or questions, please consider joining our free electronic forum hosted on the Willow Tree Learning website www.willowtreelearning. co.uk or join the Essential SENCO Network to further extend your thinking and professional development. In the meantime, read on and explore your own thinking about SEND intervention and how *you* can plan provision with purpose.

1. Assessment and intervention

Assessment and intervention are key phrases within the vocabulary of all educationalists, particularly, SENCOs and SEN Practitioners. **The words share an interdependency as they each inform the other.** Formative assessment, where information is gathered to inform action, *by definition*, leads to the identification of action to be taken. Summative assessment, which tends to be a measurement of prior attainment, *by implication*, informs action to be taken. After all, whether the attainment is high or low it will imply next steps. The action that is taken is of course known collectively as intervention.

The *Cambridge English Dictionary* defines intervention as: 'the action of becoming intentionally involved in a difficult situation, in order to improve it or prevent it from getting worse'. The words 'intentionally involved' are deemed to hold the greatest relevance to us in our work. As is the notion of action for improvement. **Ultimately intervention is about a planned action for positive change and SEND intervention refers to the intended actions identified to remove or overcome barriers to learning.** Intervention is, however, only one element of SEND *provision*. The *Cambridge English Dictionary* defines provision as: 'the act of providing something'.

According to these definitions, SEND intervention relates to action that is intended to improve learning and SEND provision is the overall offer of something. This 'something' could include an action with positive intent, i.e. an intervention, but it could also be the offer of support or the offer to make changes or adjustments to delivery. **It is essential that an intervention is recognised as one element of provision, but the two concepts are not interchangeable. This distinction allows SENCOs and SEN Practitioners to evaluate provision as a whole and to reflect on the intent of individual interventions as a part of their provision, along with other aspects of quality- first teaching adjustments and support.**

Interventions are frequently captured and recorded on a provision map. Indeed, it is more likely than not that you have written or have access to a provision map within

DOI: 10.4324/9781003179436-1

your school or setting. But I wonder, do you have a *provision* map or an *intervention* map? And does this really matter? The argument presented here is that yes, it does matter, and this is because, however useful a record of interventions might be, it may 'miss' some of the additional strands of provision that you offer to learners with SEND. For example, where do you capture teacher adjustments and/or the support or resources available to learners? If you are already capturing the full range of provision on your map, well done you, but if yours currently captures the interventions that are offered, it may be more appropriate to consider this as an intervention map. This is certainly true for provision maps that I have designed and recommended in the past. They often sought to capture the interventions that were offered to learners from different year groups who were experiencing particular barriers to learning, but rarely captured teacher adjustments or other forms of support available. As such, this would be a useful intervention record, but it would not fulfil its potential as a provision map.

Provision mapping in comparison to a provision map

Provision mapping as a process was intended to be an annual strategic leadership activity. According to Jean Gross (2015) there are six stages to provision mapping. The first stage involves auditing expected need for the following year. During this stage, staff are encouraged to consider and compare the projected need to the current needs of learners. This should lead to the second stage, which is to identify any anticipated changes or staff development needs. The third stage involves consideration of the SEN budget, and the fourth stage is to consider the evidence of what works in overcoming or removing barriers to learning. These four stages are intended to provide clarity regarding expected changes in cohort needs and, by implication, staffing needs, as well as offer clarity regarding budget availability, which will confirm what may be possible, and finally, a review of evidence regarding actions that may generate the greatest impact. If the first four stages are about planning, the fifth stage can be considered in relation to implementation, as this is about meeting the needs of learners with the identified provision. The final, sixth stage involves tracking progress and measuring impact, which is integrated into the next provision mapping cycle.

The provision map itself was intended to capture the findings of stages one to four and to enable additions or amendments during the year. **The risk is, however, that provision maps are generated without the strategic leadership conversations about projected needs, training, resources and what evidence** shows is most effective. **Instead, the map is completed by the SENCO and/or SEN Practitioner and often utilises the same provision that existed the year before. So instead of identifying provision to meet the needs of learners, there is a risk that learners become matched to existing provision.** The provision map may also simply become a record of interventions that are available, rather than a detailed description of diverse and personalised provision, which includes teacher adjustments, support and relevant interventions.

Teacher adjustments

Teacher adjustments refer to the 'tweaks' that staff make when teaching to enable greater access and participation for learners. For example, when a teacher or teaching assistant knows that a learner experiences reading as a barrier, then they will read to the learner rather than asking them to read text for themselves. Similarly, if they know that a learner has a small working memory, they will reduce the amount of information the learner is required to hold and may ask them to summarise key points at the end of an instruction. These are all adjustments or tweaks that the adult makes to their delivery to promote participation. These adjustments are more personalised than differentiation, which is of course an entitlement of all learners. Adjustments require effective knowledge both of the learner's individual learning profile, and options or strategies for adaptation.

Resources and support

Support is another type of provision offered in schools and settings. Support can include access to physical resources such as pencil grips, laptops, fidget toys, electronic tablets, sensory cushions, voice recorders etc., as well as support from adults or other learners when additional time is made available from the teacher, TA, peer supporter or volunteer. This support is part of the overall provision offered but is not technically an intervention on its own. When an adult is providing support, they *may* apply an intervention (an action with a positive intent), but the deployment of an adult to a group of learners is support and not intervention. The intervention evolves from the action the adult takes with the learner and its intended outcome.

As you read this you may be wondering if this is *actually* relevant to you in your role or simply a pedantic exploration of words? After all, in SEND we talk about provision, intervention, support and adjustments, but does it really matter which word is used? The argument here is that it does matter to SENCOs, SEN

Practitioners and those accountable for SEND provision, as ultimately *you* need to ensure that a balance of provision exists in your setting to be confident that learners are getting the 'best' deal. **However evidence-based an intervention is, if the learner only accesses this three times a week for 30 minutes, that is a total of 1.5 hours from a 30-hour week. It is essential that the remaining 28.5 hours are accessible to them and the content is relevant to their needs.** Similarly, no matter how effectively the teacher 'tweaks' the content or mode of delivery of the curriculum, if the learner needs provision that is additional to or different from this curriculum (such as targeted speech and language work), their speech and language needs will not be met without a targeted intervention. SEND provision needs to offer a balance of teacher adjustments, support and intervention in order to overcome and, where possible, ultimately remove, barriers to learning.

The resources that follow are intended to help you to audit the provision offered across your setting. They include a SEND intervention map and an intervention index. This is intended to help you capture the range of interventions offered in your setting and the index captures the *rationale* for application. The intervention index was originally inspired by a wonderful SENCO, who was sharing their intervention map, which included a few sessions of 'tiger club'. This sounded marvellous, as its ambiguity led me to wonder whether learners met to role-play the behaviour of tigers, or if they learnt about tigers or created junk models of tigers. In fact, it was the school's shorthand for a reading intervention group, the details of which were not able to be captured in the intervention map. Yet, by providing the description of tiger club in the intervention index, the school were able to offer clarity of purpose and rationale and it reduced the need to explain this elsewhere.

The SEND Menu of Adjustments (Teacher Tweaks) is intended to offer a useful 'starter' for teachers to use to identify the adjustments they regularly apply within their class. It is presented here as a menu of strategies linked to the Code of Practice four categories of need as well as the 7 Cs Learning Portfolio. Staff can highlight the frequently used adjustments which can be reviewed by the SENCO or SEN Practitioner. It is essential to remember, however, that once your own adjustment options are written down, this does not become a definitive list. Collectively, staff should review the list, adding in other adjustment options as they evolve, otherwise the menu can become repetitive and over time will simply lose relevance. Our menus should reflect the diversity of the adjustments and support we offer the learners we are working with at the time. As they change, so our menus must change. The menu can also be useful for identifying staff training needs, as colleagues may be prompted to seek clarification regarding the rationale or application of such approaches.

Menu of Adjustments – 4 Categories of Need

Cognition & Learning	Communication & Interaction	Social, Emotional & Mental Health	Physical &/or Sensory
• Teacher refers to alternative means of recording, (use of voice recorder, type, film.)	• Use concise language and visual prompts or models	• Agree start and finish time	• Adapt materials so more accessible
• Sufficient time for task	• Summarise key points	• Make explicit task relevance	• Scaffold tasks so skills broken into small steps
• Short 'bursts' of work	• Pre-teach key words	• Praise effort & engagement	• Adapt working position
• Step by step instructions	• Check out understanding by asking questions	• Learner & adult identifies success each day	• Reduce environmental noise and ensure sufficient light
• Teacher uses visual prompts (YouTube clip, model example, photos or picture cards)	• Explicit beginning and ending of task within agreed time limit	• Set own goal for the week	• Pre-prepare resources to support access
• Pause to ask questions	• Advanced warning of change	• Ask questions to encourage self –reflection	• Promote regular movement and posture change
• Structured choices	• Explain purpose of task	• Learner selects task order	
• Now & next structure		• Share 'I can' statements	

7 Cs Menu of Adjustments (Teacher Tweaks)

Cognition

- Concise instructions
- Chunk key information
- Ask learner to paraphrase
- Use visual prompts
- Make explicit the implicit
- Ask questions
- Provide extra time

Communication

- Combine instructions with modelled demonstration and or visual prompts
- Use of gesture, shared communication cards/aids
- Model 'my turn, your turn' structure and expectation
- Use photos and film clips
- Check out understanding at start of the session
- Remain mindful of literal language

Creativity

- Use questions to promote alternative thinking
- Model 'wondering' and 'contemplation'
- Share own examples and creative interests
- Promote self-directed learning opportunities and options for recording
- Model 'courage' and 'having a go' at something new
- Promote positive expectations and trust in learners

Control

- Integrate reminders of learning behaviour expectations
- Proximal praise
- 'Notice' and signal positive actions
- Model a language of emotions and connect to actions
- Celebrate effort and resiliency
- Informative praise and feedback

Compassion

- Monitor friendship groups and broker connections if necessary
- Teach games or activities for learners to play
- Encourage self-selection and decision making using structured choices
- Ask learners to identify what they think they have done well at that day
- Remain fair and consistent and refer to agreed class rules

Co-ordination

- Plan some tasks that do not require writing
- Notice the sensory environment, alter desk layout or adjust blinds
- Encourage standing, sitting and movement between tasks
- Model movement and encourage rehearsal
- Remind learners about posture and ensure furniture 'fits' the learner

Curriculum

- Effective differentiation with integrated personalisation where necessary
- Read written information
- Recap on learning rules
- Explicitly define the purpose of the learning and how it can be used again
- Recap on subject specific language and ensure access for all
- Adjust the curriculum is interesting and relevant for all

General

- Talking partners
- Time to think
- Hands up if...
- Quizzes
- Positive praise and encouragement
- Explicit and relevant feedback
- Learning walls and visual prompts
- Resource packs for key information

The SEND resources and support menu can be used to capture, and at times act as a reminder to Staff about, the range of resources and support that are available to them for deployment. It can also help to inform your own auditing process of existing and necessary resources. These menus also include strategies relating to the Code of Practice four categories of need as well as the 7 Cs.

The SEN intervention map (example and template) may be useful to help identify the interventions offered for learners during a half term or term. Please note that although the example presented here is fully complete, you may not be offering an intervention across all year groups as you may not have a learner with that barrier to learning in that year group, so in that case you would leave the space blank. These gaps in your intervention map can help you and governors to 'check' that you are offering provision that matches the identified need, as you can cross-reference these to your SEN record. So, to quote a phrase familiar to rail passengers, do 'mind the gap!'

The SEND costed provision map template may help you define the 'overall' provision offer for learners with SEND and help to demonstrate budget allocation and ultimately value for money. Although, please remain mindful that a fully costed provision map, containing adjustments, support and interventions could become quite unwieldy to manage (without a specific IT package.) As such you may prefer to cost the adjustments, resources/support and the interventions you offer individually and then collate the costs, instead of attempting to include it all in one document. This will be personal preference and there is not a right or a wrong way. **What is important is that you can account for *what* you do, *why* you do this and not something else, and *how* you know it makes a difference?** This level of clarity will help you to capture the information and share it with leaders, governors, your academy trust, Ofsted and your local authority if requested. You will also be able to consider including these documents within your SEN information report as a way of capturing your annual 'offer' for learners with SEND. But remember, only include adjustments, support or intervention that you *actually* provide, as if you declare your intention to provide something, 'others' (such as parents/carers, governors and Ofsted) will assume that you are. Provision maps cannot become a record of what you could, might or sometimes provide, but rather are a record of what *is* provided.

Menu of Resources and Support – 4 Categories of Need

Cognition & Learning	Communication & Interaction	Social, Emotional & Mental Health	Physical &/or Sensory
• Electronic tablet, voice recorder, camera, laptop	• Social stories	• Weekly 'story' board recording successes each day	• Headphones or ear defenders
• Cubes, counters, Numicon	• Social scenario discussion cards	• Letter to my teacher/friend/ self identifying highlights from week and next steps.	• Weighted cushion or blanket
• Writing boards, pencil grips, triangular pens	• Reading comprehension cards for discussion	• Positive rewards programme, stickers, Lego pieces	• Inflatable ball, wedge cushion,
• Post-its, notebook, whiteboard,	• Story books, film clips	• Visual timetable/now and next board	• Wobble board
• Sentence starters, word sheets, phonic cards	• Question sheets		• PE equipment, skipping rope, ball, bean bag
• Story books, TV programmes, websites	• Word lists		• Accessible scissors, pencils, pens
• Rehearse vertical, horizontal & circular shapes	• Socially Speaking activities and game		• Regular sensory walks
	• My turn, your turn games		
	• Phone conversations		

7 Cs Menu of Resources and Support

Cognition	Communication	Creativity	Control
• Paired working with Peer Mentor • Voice record key instructions for playback • Artefacts or visual resources • Partially completed writing frames or work sheets • Adult mediator to ask questions and promote reflections • Shorter task with greater time	• Visual timetable • Key word cards or paddles • Visual apparatus • Adult mediator • Peer Partner • Circle of Friends • Social Stories	• Ensure access to a range of creative resources/ materials and encourage self-selection and application • Use of personal goal-setting and positive rewards • Learning mentors ask questions to promote reflection • Access to laptops, iPads, voice recorders, film cameras for capturing ideas	• Feelings or My Choices diary • Class or individual token reward system • Feelings and or emoji cards • Adult to remind and reinforce positive choices or actions • Achievement Record/ Scrapbook of Success • Camera to capture positive experiences and success • Positive 'I can' posters • Access to a retreat space
Compassion	**Co-ordination**	**Curriculum**	**General**
• Friendship bench or bus stop • Learner interest groups • Personal Achievement Record • My thoughts bubble sheet • Class reward stickers or certificates for learners to distribute and explain why • Compliments board	• Voice recording software • Fine Motor skills rehearsal sheets – circular, vertical & horizontal lines • Dot-to-dot, jigsaws, paper chains, snowflakes, colouring & cutting tasks • Wobble board • Pencil grips, sloping board, posture cushions, weighted blankets • Ear defenders, headphones, sunglasses	• Reader pens, laptops, tablets, voice recorder, film recorders • Use of visual prompts and multimedia to aid access • Adult to mediate and pose questions • Peer Mentors and modelled examples of expectations • Reference materials to aid independent learning	• Adults to mediate and or reinforce a skill or a learning behaviour. • Visual prompts & equipment • Range of alternative recording devices • Peer grouping that provides modelled examples • Task checklists and organisation prompts

SEN Intervention Map Primary Example – Cognition & Learning

Date:

Category of Need	Barrier to Learning	Year R	Year 1	Year 2	Year 3	Year 4	Year 5	Year 6
C&L	Working Memory	I say, you say games – small group weekly	Memory group – pairs, verbal recall games twice weekly	Memory partners – digits forwards and backwards twice weekly	Working memory games twice weekly	Memory partners – digits forwards and backwards twice weekly	Mind mapping group – weekly Memory Partners twice weekly	Note-taking rehearsal – weekly, ongoing memory games
	Speed of Processing	Quick fire games – twice weekly small group	Quick fire games weekly – small group play reaction time games: snap, hungry hippos, beat the clock	Beat my score – pairs work together to complete tasks with more fluency – weekly	Quick fire games weekly – small group play reaction time games: snap, word association, select and sort	Timed response games – twice weekly	Quick fire games weekly – small group play reaction time games:	Timed response games – twice weekly
	Attention	Magic box listen and do game twice weekly	Spot the difference, can you find group games twice weekly	Listen and colour activity group twice weekly	Can you find – treasure hunt weekly following instructions	Active listening games – twice weekly	Active listening games – twice weekly	Listen and say – small group twice weekly
	Reading	Daily picture book group	Daily sounds and sight words rehearsal group	Toe-by-toe twice weekly	See and hear – twice weekly group exploring sounds	Decoding group – weekly rehearsal of reading skills	Read for meaning – weekly comprehension	Textbook reading – weekly group rehearsal
	Writing	Multi-media mark making group daily	Fine motor control group – twice weekly	Weekly letter formation rehearsal group	Vocabulary for writing group weekly	Voice recorders – weekly rehearsal to capture ideas for writing	Alternative words – group explore word meanings weekly	Communication in words – letters & diary- writing techniques
	Numbers	Animal counting – twice weekly counting group	Bigger or smaller – weekly number group	Forwards and backwards – twice weekly counting group	Multiplication group – twice weekly rehearsal	4 Functions – weekly small group rehearsing skills	4 Functions – weekly small group rehearsing skills	Money and time – weekly group rehearsing skills

SEN Intervention Map Primary Example – Communication & Interaction

Date:

Category of Need	Barrier to Learning	Year R	Year 1	Year 2	Year 3	Year 4	Year 5	Year 6
C & I	Expressive Vocabulary	Picture exchange games – small group twice weekly	New words group – twice weekly	Category words – twice weekly	New words group – twice weekly	Curriculum vocabulary – subject word group weekly	New words group – twice weekly	Curriculum vocabulary – subject word group weekly
	Articulation	Singing our sounds group – weekly	Say to play club – weekly	See it, say it group – weekly	Talking partners weekly discussion group	New words and meanings group weekly	Talking partners weekly discussion group	Finding out more – weekly group discussing types of questions
	Receptive Vocabulary	Words and pictures group – weekly vocab	What does that mean group? Weekly	Prepositions weekly group	What does that mean group? Weekly	Find the key words group – weekly	What does that mean group? Weekly	Find the key words group – weekly
	Collaborative Conversation	About me discussion group weekly	Tell me about you! Weekly discussion group	I like, do you like weekly discussion group	What do you think about…? Weekly conversation group	Let's debate – weekly discussion group	Conversation starters – weekly ice breaker group	Questions to ask – weekly group to rehearse social situations
	Listening	Words and actions group – weekly	Listen and do activity group – follow specific actions in group – weekly	Listen and do activity group – follow specific actions in group – weekly	Treasure hunt weekly group	I said, you said paired activity – weekly	Information detectives – weekly group identifying key words	Active listening helpful tips – weekly group teaching note taking
	Social Communication	Play and talk group – weekly	My turn, your turn – weekly paired game play	My space, your space group work weekly	What should I say? Small group weekly	What would you say? Social scenario group weekly	Ice breakers – small group weekly	Preparing for new situations – weekly small group
	Social Interaction	Playing alongside – paired groups twice weekly	How to win and lose a game – paired group weekly	What does that mean? Social response discussion group weekly	What would I do? Small group weekly	What does that mean? Social Scenario discussion group weekly	What might happen next? Weekly discussion group	What if discussion group – weekly

SEN Intervention Map Secondary Example – Social, Emotional & Mental Health

Date:

Category of Need	Barrier to Learning	Year 7	Year 8	Year 9	Year 10	Year 11
SEMH	Friendships	Shared interest groups – daily lunchtime club	Why did they say that? Understanding friendship dos and don'ts – weekly discussion group	Project teams – group initiative involving 4 students completing a set task for half a term	Social learning group – weekly interest group meetings	Duke of Edinburgh scheme activities
	Anxiety	Anxious thoughts – weekly discussion group linking thoughts and positive actions	Thinking bias – weekly group exploring CBT ways of thinking	Anxiety management – tools for living alongside anxiety weekly group	Positive action group – weekly meeting to try out mindfulness, Pilates, yoga	Peer coaching – teach coaching questions for use with self and others, weekly group
	Fear of Failure	Have a go group – diverse weekly activities to experience success and failure	Do it anyway – new experiences and activities introduced weekly	Coaching Conversations – weekly paired discussions and goal-setting	Planning for my success – small group discussion, focus on short-term goals and steps for achievement	What's next for me? – small group to plan transition and mitigate associated risks
	Self-efficacy	Mission impossible – weekly small group explore scenarios and projects making decisions and considering consequences.	My Achievement Record – scrapbook of achievements at school, home and out and about. Fortnightly updates with group	Positive action group – weekly meeting to try out mindfulness, Pilates, yoga	My Achievement Record – scrapbook of achievements at school, home and out and about. Fortnightly updates with group	Good endings lead to good beginnings – weekly group to reflect on years at school, achievements, success and set goals for next steps
	Anger	Warning signs – weekly discussion group to identify feelings and actions for management	Coaching conversation – weekly paired discussion identifying hopes and fears -	Anger management techniques – weekly group to explore visualisations, mindfulness, self-talk, retreat	Asking for help –weekly small group rehearsing how to ask for support and to stay calm	Life-long management – weekly discussion group on strategies for use in workplace, home environment, social situations

SEN Intervention Map Secondary Example – Physical and Sensory

Date:

Category of Need	Barrier to Learning	Year 7	Year 8	Year 9	Year 10	Year 11
P/S	Fine Motor Skills	This might help – weekly group to explore alternative means of recording and rehearse skills of use	Get creative – weekly lunchtime club completing activities that rehearse fine motor skills	Charity wrap – weekly group to wrap presents and prepare parcels for local charity	Skills Rehearsal group – weekly lunchtime group rehearsal of cutting, slicing, peeling, sewing and other life skills	Skills analysis audit – weekly paired opportunity to evaluate strengths and areas of difficulty to inform future planning
	Gross Motor Skills (Co-ordination)	Ball skills – weekly lunchtime club to rehearse kicking, catching, throwing etc	Posture and stability workshop – weekly group rehearsing supportive techniques	Fitness and co-ordination group – weekly outdoor games rehearsing skills and fluency of movements	Sports for life – weekly group to explore activities that rehearse skills and could be maintained into adulthood	Sports for life – weekly group to explore activities that rehearse skills and could be maintained into adulthood
	Sensory Processing	Sensory self-evaluation – weekly paired activity to audit own perception of sensory experiences and try out actions to help	Sensory scenario group – weekly discussion of sensory experiences associated with shopping, days out, weather changes	Sensational study skills – weekly small group discussion of sensory overload associated with studying and techniques for management	Sensational study skills – weekly small group discussion of sensory overload associated with studying and techniques for management	Sensory scenario group – weekly discussion of sensory experiences associated with workplaces, share thoughts and techniques for management
	Mobility	Mobility self-evaluation – individual analysis of need, identifying strengths and areas for development. Weekly rehearsal of skills identified for improvement.	Individual physio plan as required	Individual physio plan as required	Individual physio plan as required	Individual physio plan as required
	Hearing and Vision	Sensory self-audit – individual analysis of need and support. Weekly rehearsal of skills or support as required.	Individual sensory support plan as required	Individual sensory support plan as required	Individual sensory support plan as required	Individual sensory support plan as required

SEN Intervention Map Primary Template

Date:

Category of Need	Barrier to Learning	Year R	Year 1	Year 2	Year 3	Year 4	Year 5	Year 6

SEN Intervention Map Secondary Template

Date:

Category of Need	Barrier to Learning	Year 7	Year 8	Year 9	Year 10	Year 11

Willow School Intervention Index Cognition & Learning

Intervention	What Is It?	Why Use It?	With Whom?	How Often?	Anticipated Impact?	Actual Impact?
Working Memory Activities Phases 1–6	Structured activities increasing in complexity. Including, digit recall, missing objects,	Working memory	Groups of 6 pupils with a small working memory or experiencing difficulties holding information	Weekly for 30 minutes with additional adult mediator	Increased confidence, improved strategies for recalling information	
Reaction Time Games 1–3	Whack a mole, beat the clock and follow my lead are some of the games that are played.	Speed of processing	Pupils race against their own times, in groups of 4	Twice weekly for 15 minutes	Greater fluency and accuracy. Increased confidence to try to work quickly.	
Quickly Find	Variety of tasks involving speed and location.	Speed of processing	Pupils race against their own times, in groups of 4	Twice weekly for 15 minutes.	Greater fluency and accuracy. Increased confidence to try to work quickly.	
Listen & Do	Pupils follow instructions from an adult or another peer to complete a specific task.	Listening and attention	Groups of up to 6 pupils	Weekly for 30 minutes with additional adult mediator	Increased accuracy and attention to key words and instructions.	
Spot the Difference	Pupils are shown similar visual pictures and asked to identify the differences.	Promote visual discrimination	Groups of up to 6 pupils	Twice weekly for 15 minutes	Increased accuracy and attention to visual information.	
Active Listening Games	Adult tells a story or provides key information relating to a scenario, and pupils have to answer questions.	Promote listening skills and auditory retention	Groups of up to 6 pupils	Twice weekly for 15 minutes	Increase accuracy and attention to verbal information and instructions.	

Willow School Intervention Index Communication & Interaction

Intervention	What Is It?	Why Use It?	With Whom?	How Often?	Anticipated Impact?	Actual Impact?
Category of Words	Sorting pictures in to categories and adding new and known vocabulary in to categories. Develop pupil word folder to aid writing.	Develop and organise expressive vocabulary	Groups of 6 pupils with an adult	Weekly for 30 minutes with additional adult mediator	Increased vocabulary for use in speech and writing	
Prepositions	Play games and follow instructions involving in, on, under, above, next to	Language development	Individual pupils with SALT	Twice weekly for 15 minutes	Greater understanding of language.	
Can I Play?	Role play social situations with children initiating contact for play	Social communication & play	Up to 4 pupils in group with adult	Weekly for 30 minutes with additional adult during lunch time	Greater use of language to initiate play with peers.	
Find the Key word	Pupils highlight written information identifying words that help them understand	Vocabulary and inference	Groups of up to 6 pupils	Weekly for 30 minutes with additional adult mediator	Increased accuracy and attention to key words and instructions.	
Conversation Starters	Rehearse 'ice breakers' and conversation starters in different social scenarios.	Promote social communication and social interaction skills	Groups of up to 4 pupils	Weekly for 30 minutes with additional adult	Increased confidence in social situations and greater use of verbal communication.	
My Space, Your Space	Social stories and role play to illustrate socially appropriate interaction	Promote social communication and personal safety	Groups of up to 4 pupils	Weekly for 30 minutes with additional adult	Increase awareness of personal space, greater ability to sit on carpet or in the dining hall.	

Willow School Intervention Index Social, Emotional & Mental Health

Intervention	What Is It?	Why Use It?	With Whom?	How Often?	Anticipated Impact?	Actual Impact?
Board Game Friday	Pupils play board games having read and agreed the instructions and established a system for turn-taking.	Turn-taking, listening, attention	Groups of 4 pupils	Weekly for 30 minutes with additional adult mediator	Increased turn-taking and negotiation skills	
Worry Box	Pupils explore the content of a worry box and discuss actions that could be taken to manage these worries.	Promote problem solving, and alternative thinking	Groups of up to 6 pupils	Weekly for 30 minutes with additional adult mediator	Greater resilience, confidence and experience of problem solving	
About Me	Pupils complete a scrap book with information about themselves, their likes and dislikes	Promote self-awareness, self-esteem and confidence	Groups of up to 4 pupils	Weekly for 30 minutes with additional adult mediator	More confidence to express a preference or give a view. Increase in positive comments about self	
Our Project	Pupils have an opportunity to work together to plan and research a project	Team building, listening, turn-taking	Groups of up to 6 pupils	Weekly for 30 minutes with additional adult mediator	Increased skills of negotiation, turn-taking and confidence.	
Yes I Can	Pupils complete a range of non-curriculum challenges and identify their success	Promote confidence and success	Groups of up to 6 pupils	Twice weekly for 15 minutes	Increased confidence and efficacy	
My Feelings	Pupils explore feelings in themselves and others	Promote a language for feelings linked to social scenarios	Groups of up to 6 pupils	Weekly for 30 minutes with additional adult mediator	Increase use of verbal description of feelings. Greater emotional awareness of self and others	

Willow School Intervention Index Physical & Sensory

Intervention	What Is It?	Why Use It?	With Whom?	How Often?	Anticipated Impact?	Actual Impact?
Sensory Circuits	Structured activities increasing in complexity. Follow programme from "Sensory Circuits" by Jane Horwood	Develop fluency and accuracy of movements	Groups of 6 pupils with an additional adult.	Twice weekly for 20 minutes with additional adult mediator	Increased co-ordination, organisation and sequencing skills	
Copy Me	Rehearsal of vertical, horizontal and circular movements with a pen, pencil, chalk and paint brush. 'Leader' draws and partner copies, then pupils swap.	Fine motor control and accuracy	Pupils work in pairs – up to 6 in a group	Twice weekly for 15 minutes	Greater fluency and accuracy and improved letter formation and handwriting	
Individual Physio Programme	Specific programme of exercises prepared by Physiotherapist	Core muscle strength and control	Individual pupil	Twice weekly for 15 minutes.	Greater fluency and accuracy. Increased movement	
Cut n Paste	Each week there is a different theme or topic, that Pupils find images and pictures to create a group collage.	Fine motor skills including scissor control	Groups of up to 6 pupils	Weekly for 30 minutes with additional adult mediator	Increased accuracy and fluency of fine motor skills	
Hop, Skip and Jump	Pupils engage in a follow the leader physical programme involving controlled physical movements around an obstacle course.	Promote co-ordination and controlled movements	Groups of up to 6 pupils	Twice weekly for 15 minutes	Increased accuracy and fluency of movements.	
Jewellery Making	Pupils refine threading and fine motor skills to create beaded jewellery	Promote fine motor skills	Groups of up to 6 pupils	Weekly for 30 minutes with additional adult mediator	Increase in fluency and control of pincer grip	

Intervention Index Cognition & Learning

Intervention	What Is It?	Why Use It?	With Whom?	How Often?	Anticipated Impact?	Actual Impact?

Intervention Index Communication & Interaction

Intervention	What Is It?	Why Use It?	With Whom?	How Often?	Anticipated Impact?	Actual Impact?

Intervention Index Social, Emotional & Mental Health

Intervention	What Is It?	Why Use It?	With Whom?	How Often?	Anticipated Impact?	Actual Impact?

Intervention Index Physical & Sensory

Intervention	What Is It?	Why Use It?	With Whom?	How Often?	Anticipated Impact?	Actual Impact?

SEND Costed Provision Map – Cognition & Learning Primary Example

Barrier to Learning	Type of Provision	Reception	Year 1	Year 2	Year 3	Year 4	Year 5	Year 6
Working Memory	Adjustments	Provide a visual example (model)	Simple language combined with modelled example	Simple language and learner paraphrases instructions	Simple language and learner paraphrases instructions	Talking partners summarise key points to each other	Verbal scaffolding with visual prompt to summarise	Verbal scaffolding with visual prompt to summarise
	Support	Use of visual symbols or signs	Use of visual symbols, adult mediator works with a group	Teacher records instructions to be played back –group support from TA	Learner voice records instructions to play back for self, TA reinforces skill	Key points provided in writing or as a mind map for learner to use, TA reinforces skill	Mind Mapping templates given for own recording	Note taking templates given for own recording
	Intervention	Teach usage of symbols and signs and play matching game 4 × 15 minutes per week	Auditory memory games 4 × 15 minutes per week	Working Memory activity group 3 × 20 minute per week	Working Memory activity group 3 × 20 minute per week	Working Memory activity group 3 × 20 minute per week	Mind Mapping and memory games activity group 3 × 20 minutes per week	Note taking and memory games activity group 3 × 20 minutes per week
	Cost	TA cost £12 per hour Termly cost = £144	£12 per hour Termly cost = £144 plus TA support 3 hours in class, £36 daily cost termly cost = £2,160	£12 per hour Termly cost = 144 plus TA support 3 hours in class, £36 daily cost termly cost = £2,160	£12 per hour Termly cost = £144 plus TA support 3 hours in class, £36 daily cost termly cost = £2,160	£12 per hour Termly cost = £144 plus TA support 3 hours in class, £36 daily cost termly cost = £2,160	£12 per hour Termly cost = £144	£12 per hour Termly cost = £144

Barrier to Learning	Type of Provision	Reception	Year 1	Year 2	Year 3	Year 4	Year 5	Year 6
Phonics & Phonological Awareness	**Adjustments**	Use of visual symbols and actions	Refer to visual prompt of letters with picture cue	Direct instruction of letter sounds with visual prompt	Teacher reads written information	Teacher reads written information	Teacher and Learner share reading of key text	Teacher and Learner share reading of key text
	Support	Going on a sound hunt – TA takes group to look for objects beginning with the same sound	Use of personalised letter card with picture prompts and letter tiles	Use personalised letter sheet and word building folder	Use personalised letter sheet and word building folder	Key letter and word sheet, pre teaching of subject vocabulary	Key letter and word sheet, pre teaching of subject vocabulary	Pre teaching of Subject vocabulary sheet
	Intervention	Individual matching of sounds and letter identification 4 × 15 minutes per week	Sounds and object game – matching and sorting according to sounds 4 × 15 mins weekly	Synthesis and Segmentation of 2 and 3 letter words 4 × 15 minutes per week	Visual word building with 15 letter sounds 4 × 15 minutes per week	Visual word building with 26 letter sounds 4 × 15 minutes per week	Personalised phonics programme 3 × 20 minutes per week	Personalised phonics programme 3 × 20 minutes per week
	Cost	£12 per hour Termly cost = £144	£12 per hour Termly cost = £144	£12 per hour Termly cost = £144	£12 per hour Termly cost = £144	£12 per hour Termly cost = £144	£12 per hour Termly cost = £144	£12 per hour Termly cost = £144

(Continued)

SEND Costed Provision Map – Cognition & Learning (*Continued*) Primary Example

Barrier to Learning	Type of Provision	Reception	Year 1	Year 2	Year 3	Year 4	Year 5	Year 6
Fear of Failure	**Adjustments**	Teacher praises success when seen	Use of structured choice answers, praise selection	Use of structured choice answers, praise selection	Teacher gives advanced notice of question and returns to pair of learners	Teacher asks learner and partner joint question, praise both	Teacher gives advanced notice of question and returns to learner	Teacher asks learner to ask a relevant question to others
	Support	Adults praise and encourage	Now and Next structure & positive reward	Now and Next structure & positive reward	5 'lives' introduced for each task	5 'lives' introduced for each task	Peer mentors to coach and encourage	Peer mentors to coach and encourage
	Intervention	"I can" music game listing strengths 3 × 20 mins weekly	About me group work – identify strengths – 3 × 20 mins week	Me now, me next group – identifying learning goals 3 × 20 mins wk	My 7 Cs Learning Portfolio activity group 2 × 30 mins wk	My 7 Cs Learning Portfolio activity group 2 × 30 mins wk	Coaching conversation to identify own goals 2 × 30 mins wk	Coaching conversation to identify own goals 2 × 30 mins wk
	Cost	£12 per hour Termly cost = £144	£12 per hour Termly cost = £144	£12 per hour Termly cost = £144	£12 per hour Termly cost = £144	£12 per hour Termly cost = £144	£12 per hour Termly cost = £144	£12 per hour Termly cost = £144

SEND Costed Provision Map – Communication & Interaction Secondary Example

Barrier to Learning	Type of Provision	Year 7	Year 8	Year 9	Year 10	Year 11	Year 12	Year 13
Social Communication	Adjustments	Teacher provides structured choices when asking questions	Teacher models expectations and checks out understanding	Greet learner, check in with them at regular intervals	Agrees method of communication with learner	Teacher asks learner how they can best support them	Teacher asks learner how they can best support them	Teacher asks learner how they can best support them
	Support	Access to named person, help me card, and lunchtime space	Access to named person, help me card and lunchtime space	Question prompt sheet, access to named person	Access to named person and individual learning space	Access to named person and individual learning space	Access to Individual learning space	Access to Individual learning space
	Intervention	Social Stories to rehearse new scenarios 30 mins × 2 weekly	'Asking questions' group activity 30 mins × 2 weekly	Action and Consequence group activity 30 mins × 2 weekly	Preparation for the work place – group activity linked to ice breakers at work – 30 × 2 mins weekly	Preparation for exams and interviews – group activity– 30 mins × 2 weekly	Personalised coaching and preparation for life at work or college – 1 hour weekly	Personalised coaching and preparation for life at work or college – 1 hour weekly
	Cost	£12 per hour Termly cost = £216	£12 per hour Termly cost = £216	£12 per hour Termly cost = £144	£12 per hour Termly cost = £216	£12 per hour Termly cost = £216	£12 per hour Termly cost = £216	£12 per hour Termly cost = £216

(Continued)

SEND Costed Provision Map – Communication & Interaction (*Continued*)
Secondary Example

Barrier to Learning	Type of Provision	Year 7	Year 8	Year 9	Year 10	Year 11	Year 12	Year 13
Social Interaction	Adjustments	Teacher makes explicit the implicit – clarifying what and why	Teacher makes explicit the implicit – clarifying what and why	Teacher checks in with learner throughout session	Teacher asks closed questions to learner	Advanced warning of change	Advanced notice of work expectations at start of lesson	Advanced notice of work expectations at start of lesson
	Support	Time out card to access safe and quiet space	Please say that again card	Peer work buddy	Visual study planner	Visual revision planner	Personalised questions note book	Personalised questions note book
	Intervention	Social Scenarios and consequences group activity 30 mins × 2 weekly	'What if' group activity exploring reactions 30 mins × 2 weekly	'What might happen' scenario group activity 30 mins × 2 weekly	Interactions at work – what to expect activity group 1 hour per week	Exams and interviews what to expect activity group – 1 hour per week	Personalised Coaching and Reflections group 1 hour per week	Personalised Coaching and Reflections group 1 hour per week
	Cost	£12 per hour Termly cost = £216	£12 per hour Termly cost = £216	£12 per hour Termly cost = £216	£12 per hour Termly cost = £216	£12 per hour Termly cost = £216	£12 per hour Termly cost = £216	£12 per hour Termly cost = £216
Attention	Adjustments	Concise language, ask learner to paraphrase	Series of short tasks, with options to change posture	Series of short tasks, with options to change posture	Concise instructions and short tasks integrating own interest activities	Concise instructions and short tasks integrating own interest activities	Check out understanding by asking learner to paraphrase key information	Check out understanding by asking learner to paraphrase key information

Barrier to Learning	Type of Provision	Year 7	Year 8	Year 9	Year 10	Year 11	Year 12	Year 13
	Support	Access to a work station or headphones to screen out distractions	Access to standing desk and or seating desk	Access to standing desk and or seating desk	Own interest activity book and record of achievement	Own interest activity book and record of achievement	Use of voice recorder and mind maps to aid recall and focus	Use of voice recorder and mind maps to aid recall and focus
	Intervention	What's different activity group – target visual attention to detail 30 mins weekly	Mission Impossible activity group – listen to instructions and complete task, 30 minutes weekly	Mission Impossible activity group – listen to instructions and complete task, 30 minutes weekly	Key words activity group – rehearse identification of key words from spoken language, 30 minutes weekly	Key words activity group – rehearse identification of key words from spoken language, 30 minutes weekly	Skills for self directed study and revision activity group, 30 minutes weekly	Skills for self directed study and revision activity group, 30 minutes weekly
	Cost	£6 per week Termly cost £108	£6 per week Termly cost £108	£6 per week Termly cost £108	£6 per week Termly cost £108	£6 per week Termly cost £108	£6 per week Termly cost £108	£6 per week Termly cost £108

SEND Costed Provision Map – Cognition & Learning

Barrier to Learning	Type of Provision	Year	Year	Year	Year	Year	Year	Year
	Adjustments							
	Support							
	Intervention							
	Cost							
	Adjustments							
	Support							
	Intervention							
	Cost							
	Adjustments							
	Support							
	Intervention							
	Cost							
	Adjustments							
	Support							
	Intervention							
	Cost							

SEND Costed Provision Map – Communication & Interaction

Barrier to Learning	Type of Provision	Year	Year	Year	Year	Year	Year	Year
	Adjustments							
	Support							
	Intervention							
	Cost							
	Adjustments							
	Support							
	Intervention							
	Cost							
	Adjustments							
	Support							
	Intervention							
	Cost							
	Adjustments							
	Support							
	Intervention							
	Cost							

SEND Costed Provision Map – Social, Emotional & Mental Health

Barrier to Learning	Type of Provision	Year	Year	Year	Year	Year	Year	Year	Year
	Adjustments								
	Support								
	Intervention								
	Cost								
	Adjustments								
	Support								
	Intervention								
	Cost								
	Adjustments								
	Support								
	Intervention								
	Cost								
	Adjustments								
	Support								
	Intervention								
	Cost								

SEND Costed Provision Map – Physical & Sensory

Barrier to Learning	Type of Provision	Year	Year	Year	Year	Year	Year	Year
	Adjustments							
	Support							
	Intervention							
	Cost							
	Adjustments							
	Support							
	Intervention							
	Cost							
	Adjustments							
	Support							
	Intervention							
	Cost							
	Adjustments							
	Support							
	Intervention							
	Cost							

Implications for SENCOs and SEN Practitioners

Assessment and intervention are most effective when deemed to interconnect. The assess, plan, do and review cycle promotes this connection and the 7 Cs Learning Portfolio (introduced in book 1) offers a language of assessment that includes but exceeds the curriculum. Often our shared language of assessment is that of curriculum subjects and not the skills that underpin access to the curriculum. Using the 7 Cs Learning Portfolio, SENCOs and SEN Practitioners have an opportunity to promote a consistent framework to identify learner strengths and areas for development. It is this shared language of assessment that will identify and inform relevant adjustments, support and intervention (provision) available to a learner. **The explicit identification of strengths combined with areas for development helps to focus the actions to be taken, and it is this action which becomes your SEND provision.**

Reflections

- How are you currently capturing your SEND provision?
- Do you have a provision map or is it actually an intervention map?
- Could a menu of adjustments and resources/support provide a useful starting point for staff?

References

Beating Bureaucracy in Special Educational Needs: Helping SENCOs Maintain a Work/Life Balance (2015) Jean Gross. Abingdon: Routledge.

Cambridge English Dictionary (2020a). 'Intervention'. Available at https://dictionary.cambridge.org/dictionary/english/intervention (Accessed 1 May 2021).

Cambridge English Dictionary (2020b). 'Provision'. Available at https://dictionary.cambridge.org/dictionary/english/provision (Accessed 1 May 2021).

Sensory Circuits: A Sensory Motor Skills Programme for Children (2009) Jane Horwood. LDA.

2. SEND provision with purpose

The focus of this chapter is 'SEND provision with purpose', but before exploring this, it is essential that we clarify and agree our shared definition of SEND. SEND, in this context, refers to those learners who are identified as having a special educational need and those who are disabled. As described in *SEND Assessment* (book 1 in the series), the SEND Code of Practice (2015) states that a "child or young person has SEN if they have a learning difficulty or disability which calls for special educational provision to be made for him or her" (SEND Code of Practice 2015, page 15). They continue "For children aged two or more, special educational provision is educational or training provision that is additional to or different from that made generally for other children or young people of the same age ..." (SEND Code of Practice 2015, page 16). As we know, the Code of Practice is reviewed and updated at times, so it is essential that SENCOs and SEN Practitioners are aware of the current definition of SEN, as the wording may change. However, the expectation of action will remain consistent. In many ways, it would be a far more inclusive system if we 'deleted' the word 'special' from SEN and focused on *educational* needs, as all learners have educational needs and the professionals that meet educational needs are of course teachers! That said, as long as there is a system of difference, it is essential that SENCOs and SEN Practitioners are confident in the definition of difference. Right now, in the current system, the important issue for SENCOs and SEN Practitioners is to remember that **every time we identify a learner as having SEN, we are saying that they require provision that is 'additional to or different from' that made generally for others of the same age. So, by implication, we should always be able to identify what the 'extra' provision looks like.**

The Equality Act 2010 states that a person is disabled if they have "a physical or mental impairment which has a long-term and substantial adverse effect on their ability to carry out normal day-to-day activities" (SEND Code of Practice 2015, page 16). The law defines long-term as one year and one day and substantial as 'not trivial'. This definition also refers to the impact of the impairment on day-to-

DOI: 10.4324/9781003179436-2

day activities, so a person is not necessarily disabled because they have a diagnosed impairment, it is the long term and substantial impact that the impairment has on day-to-day activities that determines identification. For example, if a learner has asthma but only occasionally uses their inhaler they may not be disabled under the act. But a learner with asthma who has to take medication twice a day and remain mindful of weather conditions which could limit their ability to go outside, is likely to be disabled under the act, as this is long-term, substantial and impacts on day-to-day activities. **The implication of this on identification, is that the term SEND can in fact, refer to three groups of learners. Those with SEN, those who are disabled and those who have SEN *and* are disabled.** Readers of book 1 will also recall the clarification of learners with medical needs as a further group. The Children and Families Act 2014 requires maintained schools and academies to make arrangements to support pupils with medical needs. A medical need may or may not become a disability, depending on whether the need becomes "long-term" and has a "substantial adverse effect". In reality, SENCOs and SEN Practitioners are required to define the SEND profile of their school or setting, which will include the identification of those learners with SEN, those who are disabled, those with SEN *and* who are disabled and those with medical needs. The SEND Profile Venn Diagram below (originally published in book 1) can be useful for capturing this information. **Knowledge of the SEND profile of learners in your setting is the foundation to planning provision with purpose.**

SEND Profile

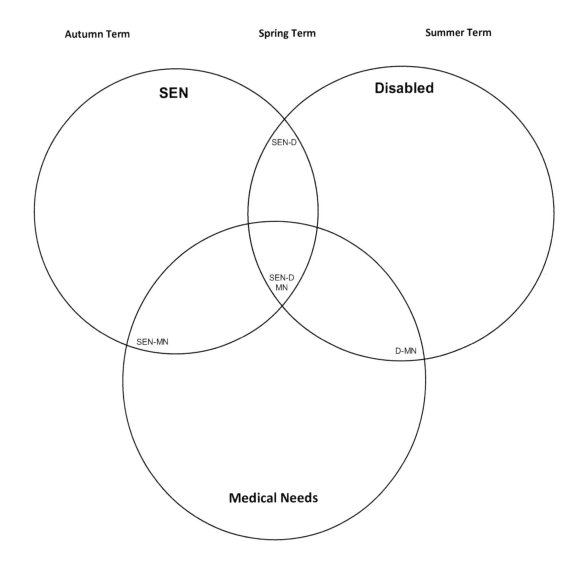

Key Definitions:

"A child has a special educational need if they have a learning difficulty that requires special educational provision." (Code of Practice 2015)

A person is disabled if they have "a physical or mental impairment which has a long-term and substantial adverse effect on their ability to carry out normal day-to-day activities'. (Equality Act 2010)

The rationale for identification

The rationale for identifying learners with SEN, D and/or medical needs is to inform action taken. It is this action that becomes the provision that is offered. For learners with SEN, the Code of Practice (2015) expects action to be 'additional to or different from' that offered to others of the same age. With regards to learners who are disabled, the Equality Act (2010) requires that we do not directly or indirectly 'discriminate, victimise or harass', linked to a protective characteristic, in this case disability. In the case of a disabled person, we must also make 'reasonable adjustments', including the provision of auxiliary aids and services. This duty is anticipatory in nature, requiring advanced thought and planning to ensure that a disabled learner is not treated less favourably or placed at disadvantage. The public sector equality duty of the Equality Act 2010 also states that

> when carrying out their functions, (they) must have regard to the need to eliminate discrimination, promote equality of opportunity and foster good relations between disabled and non-disabled children and young people. Public bodies must publish information to demonstrate their compliance with this general duty and must prepare and publish objectives to achieve the core aims of the general duty.
>
> (SEND Code of Practice 2015, page 17)

You will be aware that your school or setting has an accessibility plan which sets out how your school plans to increase access for disabled pupils to the curriculum, the physical environment and to information. Yes, you really did read, access to the *curriculum, physical environment* and, access to *information*. I reiterate this because, to many of us, the accessibility plan is often associated with physical access, which clearly is very important, but it is not the only requirement. It is essential that a disabled learner can access the building, but once they are in the building, they also need to be able to access the learning opportunities too! It may be interesting for you to review your accessibility plan (which will be published on your school website) and consider *how* you are promoting curriculum access and access to information for disabled learners, which could of course include disabled learners who also have SEN. You may also want to consider whether there is any correlation between your curriculum statement of intent and your accessibility plan. For those disabled learners who also have SEN, you might want to consider if the information in the accessibility plan links with your SEN information report. As for those learners with medical needs, we know that the action required following identification is to meet the learner's medical needs and capture our intended action in an individualised health care plan. **The similarity between all of these actions is the intention to overcome or remove barriers to learning.**

Overcoming and removing barriers to learning

Those of you familiar with book 1 will know that a distinction was made between actions taken that attempt to 'overcome' a barrier to learning and those that attempt to 'remove'. The example given was in relation to a pupil with reading as a barrier to learning. During a science lesson, the action may be to 'overcome' the barrier to learning so the learner can access the science task. In real terms this could be achieved by providing a peer or adult reader, or for the teacher to provide verbal and not written instructions. However, at some point, action will be taken that tries to teach the learner to read independently, thus 'removing' the barrier to learning. Of course, it is important to note that some barriers to learning cannot be removed. In this situation, the focus of action would be to empower the learner to 'overcome' the barrier or barriers they experience.

The effective identification of barriers to learning is at the heart of SEND assessment. It is essential that the presentation of difficulties linked to a curriculum subject is explored and understood in terms of the skills that are required for curriculum access. For example, if a learner is experiencing difficulties with maths, it is not sufficient to declare that maths is a barrier to learning, and assume the learner simply needs more maths. (Of course, the curriculum entitlement of every learner means that they will continue to receive more maths anyway.) But alongside this, it is essential that consideration is given to *why* maths is difficult for that learner? What are the skills associated with tasks in maths that are currently limiting their individual access? These could include, working memory, which is the ability to hold and manipulate information, or speed of processing as well as language, listening or attention. There are so many reasons why a learner may experience maths as a barrier to learning that an individualised approach to assessment is required. Often however, the only language of assessment available to teachers is the language of the curriculum, which is why, in book 1, the 7 Cs Learning Portfolio was introduced.

The 7 Cs Learning Portfolio

The 7 Cs Learning Portfolio provides a *language* of assessment. It enables staff, learners and their families to talk about strengths and areas for development. As the name suggests, it is a framework that includes seven concepts beginning with the letter C. Curriculum is at the centre, but it also includes cognition, communication, creativity, control, compassion and co-ordination. Within each of these, seven skills are identified so in effect, the 7 Cs provides a framework of 49 skills that can be considered as learner strengths and/or areas for improvement.

The identification of these strengths and areas for development should inform the nature of the provision that is required for that learner, both in terms of adjustments, support and intervention options. Understanding the barriers to learning experienced by learners, not only informs the nature of the provision to be offered but also directs the distribution of funding, at least it should.

SENCOs and SEN Practitioners need to be aware of the SEND funding that their school or setting receives. This is not always the same as knowing the budget you have been allocated, it is about knowing the overall income that the school receives to fund learners with SEND. Each local authority has its own system for the distribution of funding, in accordance with government guidelines, and it is essential that SENCOs and SEN Practitioners find out about this. Understanding the national and local expectations regarding the spend for supporting learners at SEN Support and those with an Education, Health and Care Plan is vital, especially if these expectations do not correlate with the funds that are available. **As SEN budgets are not ring-fenced, SENCOs and SEN Practitioners may discover a discrepancy between the LA expectation of funds available and the school reality.** SENCOs and SEN Practitioners should pursue any discrepancies and continue to champion the purpose of the SEN budget with leaders, protecting its distribution. Similarly, SENCOs and SEN Practitioners may discover that provision demands exceed their allocated budget and seek to request top up funding from the LA or indeed from governors or trustees. Once again, the SENCO and SEN Practitioner will be championing the needs of learners and will be required to justify the value for money of this spend, linked to impact and improved outcomes. Whichever, situation you find yourself in, knowing the SEN budget and expectations of others is essential. It is also often one of the hardest requirements, but stay with it, keep asking questions and track the source of funding.

7 Cs Learning Portfolio

Cognition

- Working Memory
- Speed of Processing
- Inference
- Anticipation
- Reflection
- Evaluation
- Analysis

Communication

- Speech - Expressive Vocab
  - Articulation
- Language - Understanding Vocab
- Collaborative Conversation
- Listening - Follow Instructions
- Social Communication (Output)
- Social Interaction (Input)

Curriculum

- English ➤ Reading
  ➤ Writing
  ➤ Spelling
  ➤ Number
  ➤ Shape/Space
- Maths
- Science
- Art & Music
- History & Geography
- Computing
- PE & Sport

Creativity

- Generate Ideas
- Problem Solving
- Attention
- Motivation
- Making Things
- Courage-Determination
- Trust

Co-ordination

- Fine Motor - Handwriting, Cutting, Threading
- Gross Motor - Jumping, Hopping, Kick, Catch, Throw a Ball
- Sensory – vision, hearing, tracking
- Mobility
- Stability + Balance
- Posture
- Sensory Processing

Control

- Self-regulation
- Behaviour for Learning
- Anxiety Management
- Confidence
- Resilience
- Language of Emotions
- Independence

Compassion

- Friendships
- Turn-taking
- Empathy
- Sense of Justice
- Self-esteem & Wellbeing
- Self-efficacy
- Support for Others

'Follow the money' is essential advice for SENCOs and SEN Practitioners, regarding planning provision with purpose, as you need to know what aspects of provision are funded by the SEN budget, the overall school budget and other sources such as pupil premium, in order to account for the spend and impact. The funding summary overleaf is intended to help you capture the funding available and to ensure that the deployment of funds 'matches' your SEN profile information. For example, if your greatest areas of need link to communication and interaction, the largest amount of spending should also be to overcome or remove barriers to learning linked to communication and interaction. If your evaluation reveals that funds are deployed into provision for cognition and learning, this needs to be reconsidered.

SEN Funding Budget Summary Primary

Year:

Completed by:

SEN Profile:

SEN Numbers & Percentages	Early Years	Key Stage 1	Key Stage 2	Total
EHCP				
SEN Support C&L				
SEN Support C&I				
SEN Support SEMH				
SEN Support P&S				

SEN Budget:

Additional or Top Up SEN Funding:

Expenditure	Cost	Percentage of Budget
Technology		
Adaptive equipment		
Additional Adults		
CPD		
Auxiliary Aids		
Books		
Intervention Materials		
Specialist Assessment		
Other		

Additional Information:

SEN Funding Budget Summary Secondary

Year:

Completed by:

SEN Profile

SEN Numbers & Percentages	Key Stage 3	Key Stage 4	Sixth Form	Total
EHCP				
SEN Support C&L				
SEN Support C&I				
SEN Support SEMH				
SEN Support P&S				

SEN Budget:

Additional or Top Up SEN Funding:

Expenditure	Cost	Percentage of Budget
Technology		
Adaptive equipment		
Additional adults		
CPD		
Auxiliary aids		
Books		
Intervention materials		
Specialist assessment		
Other		

Additional Information:

As mentioned in the previous chapter, you can create a costed provision map or costed adjustment menu, resources/support menu and a costed intervention map to help capture your overall provision offer, but at times you may want to create an individual personalised provision plan (PPP) for a learner. It is important to stress that it may not be appropriate or feasible to do this with all your learners, but for those where you want to track provision more closely for a period of time (perhaps to help inform a referral for an education, health and care needs assessment, or to monitor the impact of provision as part of your quality assurance activities), this could be useful. It is presented here as a personalised provision plan for an individual learner, but it could also be adapted as a PPP for a class or small group. This may be particularly useful for a supply teacher as well as a useful reminder for staff. You will notice that the focus of the PPP is provision. If you like this and choose to use this approach, it will form part of your assess, plan, do and review cycle but you would need to add in additional information for assess and review. Ultimately this captures the plan and do aspects of the cycle but could be extended to include greater baseline information and a review element.

Personalised Provision Plan SEN Support Example

Date completed: 18-1-21

Learner: James Cooper

Year group: 4

PPP completed with: Jane Ferguson (Teacher) Chloe Cooper (Mum) David Cooper (Dad) James

SEN Support category of need:

Cognition & Learning   Communication & Interaction   Social, Emotional & Mental Health   Physical &/or Sensory

Priority Barriers to Learning:

- Writing, reading, low confidence and motivation

Menu of Adjustments:

Cognition & Learning	Communication & Interaction	Social, Emotional & Mental Health	Physical &/or Sensory
• Teacher refers to alternative means of recording, (use of voice recorder, type, film.) • Sufficient time for task • Short 'bursts' of work • Step by step instructions • Visual prompts (YouTube clip, model example, photos or picture cards) • Pause to ask questions • Structured choices • Now & next structure	• Use concise language and visual prompts or models • Summarise key points • Pre teach key words • Check out understanding by asking questions • Explicit beginning and ending of task within agreed time limit • Advanced warning of change • Explain purpose of task	• Agree start and finish time • Make explicit task relevance • Praise effort & engagement • Learner & adult identifies success each day. • Set own goal for the week • Ask questions to encourage self-reflection • Learner selects task order • Share 'I can' statements	• Adapt materials so more accessible • Scaffold tasks so skills broken into small steps • Adapt working position • Reduce environmental noise and sufficient light • Pre-prepare resources to support access

Support/Resources Options:

Cognition & Learning	Communication & Interaction	Social, Emotional & Mental Health	Physical &/or Sensory
• Electronic tablet, voice recorder, camera, laptop • Cubes, counters, Numicon • Writing boards, pencil grips, triangular pens • Post-its, notebook, whiteboard, Sentence starters, word sheets, phonic cards • Story books, TV programmes, websites • Rehearse vertical, horizontal & circular shapes	• Social stories • Social scenario discussion cards • Reading comprehension cards for discussion • Story books, film clips • Question sheets • Word lists • Socially Speaking activities and game • My turn, your turn games • Phone conversations	• Weekly 'story' board recording successes each day • Letter to my teacher/friend/self identifying highlights from week and next steps. • Positive rewards programme, stickers, Lego pieces • Visual timetable/now and next board	• Headphones or ear defenders • Weighted cushion or blanket • Inflatable ball, wedge cushion, • Wobble board • PE equipment, skipping rope, ball, bean bag • Accessible scissors, pencils, pens • Provide sensory breaks

Personalised intervention and action suggestions:

• James will read every day and read a story to his grandparents via Zoom twice a week.
• James will write and draw his own weekly comic to share with the class during remote learning.
• James will play word bingo and word pairs with family members three times a week.

Review Date: 11–2–21 via Zoom

Personalised Provision Plan SEN Support

Date completed:

Learner:

Year group:

PPP completed with:

SEN Support category of need:

Cognition & Learning   Communication & Interaction   Social, Emotional & Mental Health   Physical &/or Sensory

Priority Barriers to Learning:

Menu of Adjustments:

Cognition & Learning	Communication & Interaction	Social, Emotional & Mental Health	Physical &/or Sensory
• Teacher refers to alternative means of recording, (use of voice recorder, type, film.) • Sufficient time for task • Short 'bursts' of work • Step by step instructions • Visual prompts (YouTube clip, model example, photos or picture cards) • Pause to ask questions • Structured choices • Now & next structure	• Use concise language and visual prompts or models • Summarise key points • Pre teach key words • Check out understanding by asking questions • Explicit beginning and ending of task within agreed time limit • Advanced warning of change • Explain purpose of task	• Agree start and finish time • Make explicit task relevance • Praise effort & engagement • Learner & adult identifies success each day • Set own goal for the week • Ask questions to encourage self-reflection • Learner selects task order • Share 'I can' statements	• Adapt materials so more accessible • Scaffold tasks so skills broken into small steps • Adapt working position • Reduce environmental noise and sufficient light • Pre-prepare resources to support access

Support/Resources Options:

Cognition & Learning	Communication & Interaction	Social, Emotional & Mental Health	Physical &/or Sensory
• Electronic tablet, voice recorder, camera, laptop • Cubes, counters, Numicon • Writing boards, pencil grips, triangular pens • Post-its, notebook, whiteboard, • Sentence starters, word sheets, phonic cards • Story books, TV programmes, websites	• Social stories • Social scenario discussion cards • Reading comprehension cards for discussion • Story books, film clips • Question sheets • Word lists • Socially Speaking activities and game • My turn, your turn games • Phone conversations	• Weekly 'story' board recording successes each day • Letter to my teacher/friend/ self identifying highlights from week and next steps. • Positive rewards programme, stickers, Lego pieces • Visual timetable/now and next board	• Headphones or ear defenders • Weighted cushion or blanket • Inflatable ball, wedge cushion, • Wobble board • PE equipment, skipping rope, ball, bean bag • Accessible scissors, pencils, pens • Provide sensory breaks

Personalised intervention and action suggestions:

Review Date:

Group Personalised Provision Plan SEN Support

Date completed:

Group of Learners involved: NP, JC, MC, TD, LO, SC

Year group: 3

Group PPP completed with: Mr Jackson (C/T) and Miss Taylor (TA)

SEN Support category of need:

Cognition & Learning   Communication & Interaction   Social, Emotional & Mental Health   Physical &/or Sensory

Priority Barriers to Learning:

- writing, reading and making connections

Menu of Adjustments:

Cognition & Learning	Communication & Interaction	Social, Emotional & Mental Health	Physical &/or Sensory
• Teacher refers to alternative means of recording, (use of voice recorder, type, film.) • Sufficient time for task • Short 'bursts' of work • Step by step instructions • Visual prompts (YouTube clip, model example, photos or picture cards) • Pause to ask questions • Structured choices • Now & next structure	• Use concise language and visual prompts or models • Summarise key points • Pre teach key words • Check out understanding by asking questions • Explicit beginning and ending of task within agreed time limit • Advanced warning of change • Explain purpose of task	• Agree start and finish time • Make explicit task relevance • Praise effort & engagement • Learner & adult identifies success each day. • Set own goal for the week • Ask questions to encourage self-reflection • Learner selects task order • Share 'I can' statements	• Adapt materials so more accessible • Scaffold tasks so skills broken into small steps • Adapt working position • Reduce environmental noise and sufficient light • Pre-prepare resources to support access

Support/Resources Options:

Cognition & Learning	Communication & Interaction	Social, Emotional & Mental Health	Physical &/or Sensory
• Electronic tablet, voice recorder, camera, laptop • Cubes, counters, Numicon • Writing boards, pencil grips, triangular pens • Post its, notebook, whiteboard, • Sentence starters, word sheets, phonic cards • Story books, TV programmes, websites	• Social stories • Social scenario discussion cards • Reading comprehension cards for discussion • Story books, film clips • Question sheets • Word lists • Socially Speaking activities and game • My turn, your turn games • Phone conversations	• Weekly 'story' board recording successes each day • Letter to my teacher/friend/self identifying highlights from week and next steps. • Positive rewards programme, stickers, Lego pieces • Visual timetable/now and next board	• Headphones or ear defenders • Weighted cushion or blanket • Inflatable ball, wedge cushion, • Wobble board • PE equipment, skipping rope, ball, bean bag • Accessible scissors, pencils, pens • Provide sensory breaks

Personalised group intervention and action suggestions:

• The group will generate a shared word list before starting individual writing tasks and use this to independently complete sentence starters.
• In pairs, the group will read each other's work and highlight any full stops and capital letters before it is handed in.
• At the end of a session, the group will verbally explain what work they completed and identify why this is useful and how they might use the skill again.

Review Date: 22–6–21

Group Personalised Provision Plan SEN Support

Date completed:

Group of Learners involved:

Year group:

Group PPP completed with:

SEN Support category of need:

Cognition & Learning   Communication & Interaction   Social, Emotional & Mental Health   Physical &/or Sensory

Priority Barriers to Learning:

Menu of Adjustments:

Cognition & Learning	Communication & Interaction	Social, Emotional & Mental Health	Physical &/or Sensory
• Teacher refers to alternative means of recording, (use of voice recorder, type, film.) • Sufficient time for task • Short 'bursts' of work • Step by step instructions • Visual prompts (Youtube clip, model example, photos or picture cards) • Pause to ask questions • Structured choices • Now & next structure	• Use concise language and visual prompts or models • Summarise key points • Pre teach key words • Check out understanding by asking questions • Explicit beginning and ending of task within agreed time limit • Advanced warning of change • Explain purpose of task	• Agree start and finish time • Make explicit task relevance • Praise effort & engagement • Learner & adult identifies success each day. • Set own goal for the week • Ask questions to encourage self-reflection • Learner selects task order • Share 'I can' statements	• Adapt materials so more accessible • Scaffold tasks so skills broken into small steps • Adapt working position • Reduce environmental noise and sufficient light • Pre-prepare resources to support access

Support/Resources Options:

Cognition & Learning	Communication & Interaction	Social, Emotional & Mental Health	Physical &/or Sensory
• Electronic tablet, voice recorder, camera, laptop • Cubes, counters, Numicon • Writing boards, pencil grips, triangular pens • Post its, notebook, whiteboard, Sentence starters, word sheets, phonic cards • Story books, TV programmes, websites	• Social stories • Social scenario discussion cards • Reading comprehension cards for discussion • Story books, film clips • Question sheets • Word lists • Socially Speaking activities and game • My turn, your turn games • Phone conversations	• Weekly 'story' board recording successes each day • Letter to my teacher/friend/self identifying highlights from week and next steps. • Positive rewards programme, stickers, Lego pieces • Visual timetable/now and next board	• Headphones or ear defenders • Weighted cushion or blanket • Inflatable ball, wedge cushion, Wobble board • PE equipment, skipping rope, ball, bean bag • Accessible scissors, pencils, pens • Provide sensory breaks

Personalised group intervention and action suggestions:

Review Date:

Implications for SENCOs and SEN Practitioners

Planning SEND provision with purpose requires clarity of needs and the identification of a diverse range of actions that can be offered, including teacher adjustments, support and interventions, intended to overcome or remove barriers to learning. It requires knowledge of funding and the budget sources available, as well as the evidence base of activities that offer the greatest impact and likelihood of improvement. SEND provision should always be defined according to need, identified by SEND assessment. It should be informed by an evidence base and chosen because of its relevance and anticipated positive impact, for that particular learner or group of learners.

Reflections

- Is our SEND provision informed by evidence of impact and learner interest and relevance?
- Do we define the purpose of our provision when planning its implementation and how is this captured?
- Is our SEN budget distributed to the greatest needs of our learners or have we become more generic in our distribution?

References

SEND Assessment: A Strengths-based Framework for Learners with SEND (2021) Judith Carter. Abingdon: Routledge Speechmark.

Special Educational Needs and Disability Code of Practice: 0 to 25 years – Statutory Guidance for Organisations which Work with and Support Children and Young People who have Special Educational Needs or Disabilities (2014; updated 2015). Department for Education and Department of Health.

3. Action with intent

As we have established, SEND provision, whether in the form of teacher adjustments, support or intervention, is targeted action with purpose and intent. The purpose being to overcome or remove a barrier to learning and improve the experience or outcome for a learner. This is ultimately *why* learners are identified as having SEN as it is anticipated that they will benefit from additional SEN support to overcome or remove barriers that are restricting learning, or indeed why some learners receive an education, health and care plan. Planning your SEND provision needs to be informed by the 'anticipated' impact of the action, which is of course the reason why you are choosing to do this in the first place. Capturing what we anticipate will be different for a learner because of the adjustment, support or intervention provided, will help to evaluate the 'actual' impact. **There is a risk however, that SEND provision is offered without clarity of anticipated impact and instead, it is offered as it has always, historically been offered in the school or setting. SEND provision can become a habit or a ritual, rather than an action with personalised intent.**

Currently SENCOs and SEN Practitioners attempt to capture the personalisation of SEND provision via the graduated approach. This establishes a cycle of assess, plan, do and review. This process requires the determination of a starting point or baseline, which informs the plan which is then implemented and reviewed. Since the introduction of the graduated approach in the Code of Practice 2014, SENCOs and SEN Practitioners have developed an array of formats for capturing this cycle, all of which have merits. Many of you will be delighted with your formats but if you are not, then the examples included in this chapter may be of interest to you. **As is so often the case, it is not the 'product' or format of the assess, plan, do and review cycle that is as important as the 'process' or conversation between the learner, family and staff as they engage in the cycle.** That is why the 7 Cs Learning Portfolio was intended to provide a shared *language* of assessment that could be used by staff, learners and their families. It is also why SENCOs and SEN Practitioners are encouraged to consider the wording of their assess, plan, do and review formats, and adopt a version that is written for the learner themselves. This will increase learner access (and indeed the access of other adults), as well as promote greater clarity of information. Alongside this, including the anticipated impact of actions at the planning stage will enable comparison with the actual impact to be discussed during the review meeting. The 'about me' form included in this chapter attempts to do this. It also seeks to assimilate relevant information gained from a one-page profile, thus reducing the need to produce

DOI: 10.4324/9781003179436-3

two documents. A one-page profile has huge potential as a communication tool, but only if it is communicated with the relevant people. So often, a one-page profile may be completed and then filed, rather than actually used to inform adjustments or communicate views. **If we are to generate any paperwork at the assess, plan, do or review stage, it must have purpose and practical application**.

Paperwork or work the paper?

We should also learn the lessons of the past. In the past (and indeed for some of you in the present), SENCOs and SEN Practitioners generated individual education plans (IEPs) as a way of capturing need and provision. Yet for many, the IEP became a bureaucratic chore, with very little purpose. The paperwork existed but was not effectively used by teachers or learners. It was written as part of a paper trail rather than a practical resource. Targets were often generic and curriculum related (rather than relevant to individual barriers to learning). For many they also tended to 'roll over' and continue into the next cycle, appearing to suggest that no progress had occurred during this time. In fact, it was more likely that progress had been made, but not necessarily in accordance with the objectives on the IEP. It is possible that no-one actually looked at the IEP targets again from the time of writing them, because the document itself was perceived to have no or limited value to the learner or teacher, outside of the termly review meeting. As you plan SEND provision with purpose in your school or setting, please do ensure that this is not the case for any paperwork that relates to your system. If you use one-page profiles, *use* them. Make them visible, encourage learners to have them on their desks or in their diaries. Create an environment where learners themselves remind staff of strategies that can help them and encourage staff to read and refer to them. If you adopt the 'about me' form or another format for assess, plan, do and review, do not just keep it in a folder or upload it on a shared electronic platform! Again, encourage learner ownership of the document so they have it to hand and ensure that staff refer to the record when planning. If you adopt a teacher adjustment menu or provide a record of resources and support, create an intervention map or a complete SEND provision map; ensure that it is *used* by staff and they share the purpose and potential of the document. Invest time in training colleagues, to establish a consistent language of SEND assessment and provision, so staff know *why* paperwork is requested and can see a purpose or application that benefits them and the learner. Above all, ensure that the actions that you take, and you ask of others, have a clear and purposeful intent. The examples that follow are intended to demonstrate the array of options that SENCOs and SEN Practitioners have regarding the presentation of information. Consider these in relation to your existing methods for capturing the graduated approach and reflect on the purpose of your documentation.

Anticipated and Actual Impact

Aspirations for My Learners at SEN Support – Autumn Term

Pupil name	What I would like to be different for them…	What is actually different…	Priority next steps

Aspirations for My Learners at SEN Support – Spring Term

Pupil name	What I would like to be different for them…	What is actually different…	Priority next steps

Aspirations for My Learners at SEN Support – Summer Term

Pupil name	What I would like to be different for them…	What is actually different…	Priority next steps

About Me

My name: *Phoebe Clarke*

My friends: *Tom, Simon, Jane, Jazka*

My age: *8 years old*

My birthday: *22-11-14*

My class: Robins Year 4

My teacher: *Mr Cooper*

People who visit me at school or who I visit...

Emma Wilson Educational Psychologist

What's important to me...

- *Music and dancing*
- *Art, especially colouring*
- *My family*

What people like and admire about me...

- *I am happy and kind*
- *I laugh a lot*
- *I have good handwriting*

How best to help me...

- *Ask me if I understand what I am doing*
- *Let me sit at the back of the room*
- *Tell me when things are going to change*

What I think I'm good at...

- *Singing and dancing*
- *Drawing cartoons*
- *Playing with my dog Poppy*

What my teacher thinks I'm good at....

- *Handwriting*
- *Thinking of ideas*
- *Noticing things around me*

What people at home think I'm good at...

- *Playing with Poppy our dog*
- *Noticing when things change*
- *Drawing and colouring*

What I would like to be good at...

- *Reading*
- *Staying calm*
- *Times tables*

Things I find tricky... *(barriers to my learning)* ASSESS

- *Expressing my feelings with words*
- *Listening to instructions*
- *Focusing on just one thing*

What I can do now... *(baseline)* ASSESS

- *I will shout and scream if I feel angry or frightened*
- *I listen for a few minutes but get distracted and lose focus*
- *I notice everything that is going on around me which can cause me to worry*

What I want to do next.... *(anticipated outcome)* PLAN

- *I want to be able to name my feelings and tell an adult how I feel*
- *I want to listen to instructions and be able to tell the teacher what I think we are doing*
- *I want to relax and feel calm in class so I can focus on my work*

What I will do to help me with this in school....
(action that is additional to or different from) DO

1. *I will make my own emoji cards and use them to label my feelings in the day*
2. *I will listen to stories and identify key words and answer questions about them and in class I will try to tell the teacher what I think I have to do from listening to the instructions*
3. *will try to wear headphones to see if this helps me screen out other noises so I can see if this makes me feel more relaxed and focused*

At home...

1. *I will use my emojis to show my feelings at home*
2. *I will play listening games with my mum and dad to see if I can remember what is said*
3. *I will listen to calming music before I go to bed and see if I can lie really still and think about happy things*

When I'm out and about...

1. *When we visit my Nan and Grandad I will take my emoji cards and explain how I have felt.*
2. *When we go food shopping I will try to remember 2 things Dad has told me from the shopping list*
3. *I will wear my headphones when we are out to see if that makes me feel more calm*

This is how I got on... *(actual outcome)* REVIEW

1. *I like my emoji cards and have been using them every day*
2. *I can listen for about 10 minutes now, but still find it hard to focus and remember.*
3. *Wearing headphones has helped me feel more calm*

What's next? *(baseline)* ASSESS

- *I will try to remember 3-part instructions*
- *I will try to work with a partner in Maths*
- *I will try to hold my thoughts rather than calling them out immediately*

About Me

My name: My friends:

My age: My birthday:

My class: My teacher:

People who visit me at school or who I visit...

What's important to me...

What people like and admire about me...

How best to help me...

What I think I'm good at...

What my teacher thinks I'm good at....

What people at home think I'm good at...

What I would like to be good at...

Things I find tricky... *(barriers to my learning)*   *ASSESS*

-
-
-
-

What I can do now... *(baseline)*   *ASSESS*

-
-
-
-

What I want to do next.... *(anticipated outcome)*   *PLAN*

What I will do to help me with this in school....
(action that is additional to or different from)   *DO*

1.
2.
3.

At home...

1.
2.
3.

When I'm out and about...

1.
2.
3.

This is how I got on... *(actual outcome)*   *REVIEW*

-
-
-
-

What's next? *(baseline)*   *ASSESS*

-
-
-

Capturing impact Example

Autumn 2021 – Cycle 1

| | Background Information | | | | | | | | Autumn 2021 – Cycle 1 | | | | | |
Pupil Name	Year Group	Code of Practice Category	Involvement of Outside Agencies	Diagnostic Label	Barriers to Learning	Baseline	Anticipated Outcome	Action to be Taken	Comments	Actual Outcomes/ Impact	Pupil Views	Parent/ Carer Views
			Information			Assess	Plan		Do	Review		
Joshua	1	SEMH	CAMHS	Attachment Disorder	Friendships	Isolated at playtime, peers afraid of him as he tends to hit children and take toys	Josh to play structured game within group of 3 pupils 4 out of 5 break times	Peer pyramid – adult input to teach game and model turn taking				
					Organisation and Independence	Unable to organise equipment to start task, requires adult support each session	Josh to go to table and select pencil and book every lesson	Visual checklist and reward for remembering				
					following instructions	Distracted on carpet, adult needs to remind him of instructions and set him to work every session	Josh to paraphrase work instructions to the C/T at start of evey lesson	C/T to ask Josh what he needs to do prior to each session				
Chloe	5	C&L		Dyslexia	Reading	26/26 letter sounds but cannot synthesise or segment sounds in words	Chloe to synthesise and segment 3 CVC words	Small group teaching of synthesis and segmentation 3 x weekly				
					Writing	Able to write key words but not connect sentences	Using sentence starters, Chloe to complete 3 sentences independently	Sentence starters to be provided for each written task, combined with key word sheet				

Capturing impact Example (*Continued*)

Autumn 2021 – Cycle 1

| | Background Information | | | | | Assess | Plan | | Do | | Review | |
Pupil/ Name	Year Group	Code of Practice Category	Involvement of Outside Agencies	Diagnostic Label	Barriers to Learning	Baseline	Anticipated Outcome	Action to be Taken	Comments	Actual Outcomes/ Impact	Pupil Views	Parent/ Carer Views
						Information						
					Working memory	Able to remember 1-part instructions	Use visual prompts to remind herself of instructions	Use of white board on the carpet to draw own cues and prompts				
Daniel	4	C & I	EP Paediatrican Speech Therapist	Autism	Working with others	Daniel becomes distressed when other pupils sit at the same table. He works alone 80% of time	Daniel will be able to work with another child for 60% of time	Daniel to invite a member of his group to sit at his work station for 5 minutes each session				
					Changing activities	Daniel will continue to work on task of his choice refusing to change activity until this is completed	Daniel to complete a task set and a reward task during each session	Introduce a now and next structure to each task, and reward task completion				
					Turn-taking	Daniel is not yet able to enage in paired activities as he cannot turn take	Daniel to be able to play a simple pairs game initially with an adult and then with a child	Rehearse 'My turn, Your turn' structure with an adult to complete a short game				
Sarah	3	P & S	Occupational Therapist	Dyspraxia	Handwriting	Can draw vertical lines from bottom to top, but not horizontal or circular. Mixing up upper and lower case	Greater fluency with horizontal and circular movements and improved letter formation	Teach circular and horizontal movements, and revise letter formation of vowels				

(*Continued*)

Capturing impact Example (*Continued*)

Autumn 2021 – Cycle 1

Pupil Name	Year Group	Code of Practice Category	Involvement of Outside Agencies	Diagnostic Label	Barriers to Learning	Baseline	Anticipated Outcome	Action to be Taken	Comments	Actual Outcomes/ Impact	Pupil Views	Parent/ Carer Views
				Background Information								
			Information			Assess		Plan	Do	Review		
					Fastenings on clothes	Can pull up a zip on her coat but not able to fasten buttons on cardigan	Independently fasten cardigan after PE	Focus on pincer grip and control via fine motor games: beads, threading and weaving				
					Drawing shapes	unable to use a ruler or draw around shapes	Sarah will be able to draw round shapes and use a ruler accurately during Maths tasks	Teach strategy for holding and controlling ruler and shapes whilst drawing round. Cut out and create shape confetti				
Harry	6	SEMH			Anger	throws work or equipment when frustrated. On average 3/5 days a week	Harry will be able to express his feelings using a rating scale	Teach RAG rating using emotion cards, discuss each emotion and associated physical sensations				
					Refuses tasks he thinks he may not be able to do	Resists requests to complete tasks every day. Says he can't do it and walks out of class	Harry to use 'self-talk' to coach himself to complete an unknown task	Adult to model language of 'self-talk' and mediation. Provide opportunities for Harry to identify success and to rehearse uncertainty safely				

Capturing Impact Template

Autumn – Cycle 1

Background Information													
Pupil Name	Year Group	Code of Practice Category	Involvement of Outside Agencies	Diagnostic Label	Barriers to Learning	Baseline	Anticipated Outcome	Action to be Taken	Comments	Actual Outcomes/ Impact	Pupil Views	Parent / Carer Views
		Information			Assess		Plan		Do		Review	

(Continued)

Capturing Impact Template (*Continued*)

Spring – Cycle 2

Barriers to Learning	Baseline	Anticipated Outcome	Action to be Taken	Comments	Actual Outcomes / Impact	Pupil Views	Parent / Carer Views
Assess		Plan		Do		Review	

Capturing Impact Template (*Continued*)

Summer – Cycle 3

Barriers to Learning	Baseline	Anticipated Outcome	Action to be Taken	Comments	Actual Outcomes/ Impact	Pupil Views	Parent/Carer Views
Assess		Plan		Do		Review	

The 7 Cs Learning Portfolio – Action Plan

Name: Jasmine Khan

School: Willow Academy

Birthday: 8-12-13

Date completed: 15-1-20

Written by: Ms Carter, Jasmine and Mrs Khan (Mum)

My Next Steps…

We will meet again on:
14th February 2020

My Review

How did I get on?

1.

My rating scale today is…

1—2—3—4—5—6—7—8—9—10

2.

My rating scale today is…

1—2—3—4—5—6—7—8—9—10

3.

My rating scale today is…

1—2—3—4—5—6—7—8—9—10

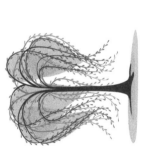

© Willow Tree Learning Ltd 2021

About Me…

Things I like:
Playing Minecraft and colouring

What I find tricky:
Reading and maths

I'm good at: *drawing and playing with my friends*

I'd like to be good at: *maths and reading*

What people like about me:

I am funny and caring and I help people.

My Strengths…

We have identified many learning strengths including these:

1. Compassion: Friendships
1—2—3—4—5—6—7—8—9—10

2 Compassion: Support for Others
1—2—3—4—5—6—7—8—9—10

3. Coordination: Fine Motor Skills
1—2—3—4—5—6—7—8—9—10

My 3 Actions to work on are…

1. **Cognition: Working Memory**
My rating scale today is…
1—2—3—4—5—6—7—8—9—10

2. *Cognition: Inference*
My rating scale today is…
1—2—3—4—5—6—7—8—9—10

3. *Curriculum: Maths*
My rating scale today is…
1—2—3—4—5—6—7—8—9—10

To help develop these skills in school I will:

1. *Join the memory club and play games twice a week for 4 weeks.*

2. *Group reading 3 times a week where I will be asked to stop and think about the story….*

3. *Use cubes to help me add on and take away numbers up to 25*

At home or when I'm out and about I will…

1. *Try to remember and collect 2 items from the shopping list*

2. *Watch a TV programme with Mum or Dad and pause it to think about what might happen next*

3. *Share out grapes with my brothers, counting out fairly*

By doing this, we hope I will be able to…

1. *Remember 2-or 3-part instructions and find ways to help me remember*

2. *Think ahead and predict what might happen next*

3. *Confidently add and takeaway up to 25*

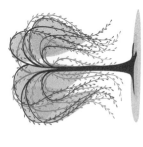

The 7 Cs Learning Portfolio – Action Plan

Name:

School:

Birthday:

Date completed:

Written by:

My Next Steps...

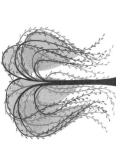

We will meet again on:

My Review

How did I get on?

1.

My rating scale today is...

1—2—3—4—5—6—7—8—9—10

2.

My rating scale today is...

1—2—3—4—5—6—7—8—9—10

3.

My rating scale today is...

1—2—3—4—5—6—7—8—9—10

About Me...

Things I like:

What I find tricky:

I'm good at:

I'd like to be good at:

What people like about me:

My Strengths...

We have identified many learning strengths including these:

1.
1—2—3—4—5—6—7—8—9—10

2.
1—2—3—4—5—6—7—8—9—10

3.
1—2—3—4—5—6—7—8—9—10

My 3 Actions to work on are...

1.

My rating scale today is...
1—2—3—4—5—6—7—8—9—10

2.

My rating scale today is...
1—2—3—4—5—6—7—8—9—10

3.

My rating scale today is...
1—2—3—4—5—6—7—8—9—10

To help develop these skills in school I will:

1.

2.

3.

At home or when I'm out and about I will...

1.

2.

3.

By doing this, we hope I will be able to...

1.

2.

3.

© Willow Tree Learning Ltd 2021

73

Learning Portfolio Priority Action Sheet

Name: Joanne Harford   School: Willow Tree School   Date Completed: 22-10-20

Completed by: Mr Jones (SENCO) Miss Leitz (C/T) Ms Harford and Jo

We have identified many learning strengths for Joanne including these:

1. **COMPASSION: Friendships** – Jo is a lovely friend and is a popular member of class
2. **CONTROL: Language of emotions** – Jo is able to talk about her feelings at home and school
3. **CO-ORDINATION – Fine motor skills** – Jo is able to write neatly and enjoys craft activities

We have agreed that the 3 actions to be worked on this half term are:

1. **COGNITION – Working memory** – we want Jo to try to hold more verbal information
2. **CURRICULUM – Reading** – Jo can read 12 letter sounds and we want her to read 20
3. **CONTROL – Anxiety management** – we want Jo to feel more confident when Mum leaves her at school

To help develop these skills in school we will:

1. **COGNITION – Working memory** – we will play verbal memory games and rehearse 2, 3 & 4 digits forwards & backwards.
2. **CURRICULUM – Reading** – Jo will work with the TA twice a day to rehearse the 12 letter sounds she knows plus 8 new sounds, using direct instruction and interleaved learning.
3. **CONTROL – Anxiety management** – Jo will set up a crafts club before school and invite some other peers to attend. Mum will drop her off at the class door.

At home we will:

1. **COGNITION – Working memory** – we will play verbal memory games such as I went shopping and will ask Jo to collect items from different rooms in the house or to collect items from the supermarket shelves when shopping.
2. **CURRICULUM – Reading** – Jo's 20 letters will be put on the fridge door and her bedroom door at home and she will read them out with Mum every day.
3. **CONTROL – Anxiety management** –Talk about the craft activity Jo will be doing at her club and agree what Jo will do at the club so she will be able to show Mum at the end of the day.

As a result, we anticipate that Joanne will be able to:

1. **COGNITION – Working memory** – Recall 3-part verbal instructions
2. **CURRICULUM – Reading** – Read 20 letter sounds
3. **CONTROL – Anxiety management** – Positively separate from Mum in the mornings.

We will meet to review this on: Wednesday 12ᵗʰ December 3.30–4pm

Learning Portfolio Priority Action Sheet

Pupil Name: **School:**   **Date Completed:**

Completed by whom:

We have identified many learning strengths including these 3:

1.

2.

3.

We have agreed that the 3 actions to be worked on this half term are:

1.

2.

3.

To help develop these skills in school we will:

1.

2.

3.

At home we will:

1.

2.

3.

As a result, we anticipate that .... will be able to:

1.

2.

3.

We will meet to review this on:

Developing staff knowledge and confidence

Investing time in supporting and developing teaching staff knowledge and confidence regarding SEND, is crucial to ensuring that action is informed by intent. **If teachers do not have a language of barriers to learning, then they do not have the foundation for identifying SEND. And quite simply, if they are not able to identify the needs of learners, they will not be able to meet those needs.** They may attempt to 'add on' suggestions that they have been told to do, but as teachers, they will not be planning personalised learning activities informed by a baseline of strengths and needs, unless they have a language that defines these. The curriculum itself does not give us a sufficient or extensive language of learning that defines strengths and barriers. It can be a wonderfully diverse knowledge bank of subjects and information, but it is not a learning portfolio, such as that of the 7 Cs. Curriculum attainment helps us to notice and measure strengths with skill application in that subject, but in itself, it does not provide a *language of skills* needed for such application. The 7 Cs Learning Portfolio attempts to provide that language. This in turn gives teachers a framework for identifying strengths and areas for development.

Knowledge of learner strengths and areas for development are the foundation for identifying actions with intent. Teachers are able to use this knowledge to identify appropriate adjustments, support and interventions that may help learners. The 7 Cs action cards that follow are intended to offer a starting point for teachers as they work with learners and their families to identify strengths and areas for development using the 7 Cs Learning Portfolio. As always, the suggestions provided are starting points. As staff confidence and knowledge increases, they may wish to develop and amend the suggestions. Please do so. You may also want to vary your application of the action cards. To begin with, teachers may choose to print or photocopy the cards back to back and use these as prompts for themselves. They can also be used during the 7 Cs Learning Portfolio meeting with the learner and their family. In this context the cards could be used to review the options for the learner to consider as their strengths and areas for development. The cards can be moved around and then selected to indicate the three strengths and the three areas for development for that learner. The teacher can then 'turn over' the three cards identified as areas for development and share the possible adjustments, support and intervention ideas. The best suggestion is to 'have a go' and vary the resources to meet your own preferences. Remember, there are no right or wrong ways to use these resources, simply possible starting points!

The 7 Cs Action Cards

Cognition

Cognition	**Working Memory**
Speed of Processing	**Inference**
Anticipation	**Reflection**
Evaluation	**Analysis**

The 7 Cs Action Cards

Cognition – Adjustment Support Intervention Ideas

Working Memory	Cognition
Adjustment: Adult remains mindful of the amount of information the learner is asked to 'hold' and checks out their understanding at the start of a session. Where possible, the adult reiterates key points using simple and concise language combined with a visual prompt of aid. **Support:** Learner uses mind maps, word sheets, visual prompts and note taking to aid recall, or records instructions to play back to self. **Intervention:** Rehearsal of auditory/visual memory skills by playing memory games to attempt to increase efficiency of recall.	

Inference	Speed of Processing
Adjustment: Adult pauses regularly to ask questions that relate to the information provided. Vary range of questions. **Support:** Model examples of how to make inferences from text or conversation and make explicit how key words triggered thoughts. Ask learners to highlight key words in text to identify the words that they could use to infer meaning. **Intervention:** Explicitly teach how to make inferences pointing out the key words used. Rehearse the skill individually with a learner or in a small group. This could also apply for social inferences using social scenarios, stories or role play.	**Adjustment:** Adult ensures the learner has sufficient time to complete the task or respond to instructions or questions. Information is broken down into smaller chunks. **Support:** Learner works with peer buddy or adult who can prompt, remind or scaffold information. Provide access to visual prompts. **Intervention:** Engage with activities that rehearse reaction time, such as hungry hippos, snap, or games that involve being quicker than before. Rehearse comprehension and extraction of key information or words from text and language.

Reflection	Anticipation
Adjustment: The adult models reflective comments and observations by integrating statements into teaching or discussion. This is explicitly labelled as reflection. **Support:** Specific and structured questions or prompts are used with an individual or small group to scaffold reflection. Visual prompts to remind the learner(s) of key details are used. **Intervention:** In pairs or small groups, adult explicitly teaches the process of reflection using questions to revisit information. Learners respond to questions prompted by an adult who may label examples of reflection.	**Adjustment:** Adult can use structured choices with a learner to encourage anticipation of preference, implications or outcome of an action. **Support:** Examples of consequences are provided to the learner who is then able to explore the likelihood of occurrence and express their own anticipated thoughts. **Intervention:** Learner works with small group of peers who ask questions of each other regarding actions and consequences. The questions could be scripted by an adult or prompted by themselves.

Analysis	Evaluation
Adjustment: Adults integrate 'what and why' type questions throughout teaching and discussion and explicitly label the process of analysis. **Support:** The management of information is scaffolded using visual or written reminders and prompts alongside questions such as "what about…?" and "why do you think this?" **Intervention:** Explicitly teach how to identify details and to focus on similarities and differences as well as relevance and impact. Scaffold the process of drawing information together to create an analysis and conclusion.	**Adjustment:** Adults create a culture of decision making where all learners are encouraged to weigh up information and express a view or preference. **Support:** Adult or peer supporters ask questions that promote exploratory thinking of advantages and disadvantages which lead to a decision or verdict. Visual prompts or photos can be used to aid recall and consideration. **Intervention:** The process of evaluation is explicitly taught individually or in a small group, working through examples and sharing process of exploration leading to a conclusion.

<u>The 7 Cs Action Cards</u>

<u>Communication</u>

Communication	**Speech – Expressive Vocabulary**
Speech – Articulation	**Language**
Collaborative Conversation	**Listening**
Social Communication (output)	**Social Interaction (input)**

The 7 Cs Action Cards

Communication – Adjustment Support Intervention Ideas

Speech – Expressive Vocabulary **Adjustment:** Adult and learner develop a non-verbal communication system such as picture or photo exchange or use gesture or other signals to enable communication. **Support:** Learner has access to visual cards or key priority word prompts to aid expressive vocabulary. Adult or peer supporter time is available to promote communication and model vocabulary. **Intervention:** Explicit teaching of key and new words to increase vocabulary. Teach category words and prepositions though individual or small group games and tuition.	**Communication**
Language **Adjustment:** Adult ensures the use of concise and accessible language, combined with visual prompts or familiar routines. Check out the learner's understanding by asking them to paraphrase work instructions at the start of an activity. **Support:** Provide opportunities for the learner to work with peer supporters who model effective language. Adults may scaffold understanding by combining verbal or written instructions with visual prompts or modelled examples. **Intervention:** Explicitly teach new vocabulary and strategies for clarifying meaning of words including asking Alexa or Siri.	**Speech – Articulation** **Adjustment:** Adult ensures the learner has sufficient time when attempting to talk. May use an agreed communication board with visual aids to support understanding. **Support:** Learner works with peer buddy or adult to rehearse articulation within conversations. Adult may help to interpret words if not understood by peers, always checking accuracy of meaning with learner. **Intervention:** Engage with activities that explicitly rehearse sound pronunciation and use of key words. Depending on age use singing, rhyme, games etc to rehearse articulation.
Listening **Adjustment:** Adult to ensure that information is concise and accessible to the learner. Provide a summary of key points and ask the learner to paraphrase. Use the learners name at the start. **Support:** Provide visual prompts or reminders of key information. Chunk information into small steps, regularly check out the learners understanding. **Intervention:** In pairs or small groups, play 'listen and do' type activities that require a specific action linked to an instruction. Use reading comprehension activities verbally and teach the identification of key words to aid understanding.	**Collaborative Conversation** **Adjustment:** Adult can use turn-taking to model and participate in conversation. If learner 'blurts out' information or interrupts, this can trigger 'my turn, your turn' structuring. **Support:** Adult may need to intervene to broker conversation with peers if learner talks at or over peers, refer to turn-taking. **Intervention:** Play structured games that teach and rehearse turn-taking and make explicit the components of a conversation through role play or observation. Rehearse social scenarios where conversations will occur and provide opportunities for the application of these skills in 'real' life.
Social Interaction (input) **Adjustment:** Adults remain responsive to comments or reactions that may appear unrelated or inappropriate. Remain calm and offer reassurance to the learner. **Support:** Ensure that the learner has access to a safe and quiet place for reflection and processing if distressed or confused by the actions of others. Attempt to label feelings expressed. **Intervention:** Explicitly teach and rehearse possible responses to social situations. Ensure the learner has an exit or closing response to say if they are unsure of what else to say, such as 'Ok then.' Introduce a circle of friends or peer supporters.	**Social Communication (output)** **Adjustment:** Adults remains responsive to comments or questions that may appear unrelated or inappropriate. Seek to 'broker' any discrepancies and relate back to the topic or thank the learner for the idea which can be discussed later. **Support:** Adult or peer supporters may seek to facilitate shared activities or joint interests to broker communication and interaction between the learner and others. **Intervention:** The explicit teaching and rehearsal of key phrases or sentence starters to aid communication in different contexts. Use social scenarios and stories to aid understanding.

The 7 Cs Action Cards

Creativity

Creativity	**Generate Ideas**
Problem Solving	**Attention**
Motivation	**Making Things**
Courage – Determination	**Trust**

The 7 Cs Action Cards

Creativity – Adjustment Support Intervention Ideas

Generate Ideas	
Adjustment: Adults may vary the modality for expressing ideas, such as the use of words, actions, Lego, pictures etc. Adult may give a prompt or an idea 'starter' that requires development and promote a culture of thinking and sharing ideas. **Support:** Provide suggestions or examples and ask questions of the learner that focus on the feasibility of an idea and express a preference. Use visual prompts or resources to fuel ideas. **Intervention:** Provide opportunities for the learner to respond to 'what could happen next?' questions and promote exploration of ideas rather than the 'right' or 'wrong' response.	**Creativity**
Attention	**Problem Solving**
Adjustment: Adult uses the learners name at the start of an instruction. Adults ensure that information is concise and is delivered with the least distractions. **Support:** Work with the learner to identify how to filter out distractions, e.g. using headphones, work stations or screens. Vary posture between tasks, e.g. sitting, standing, leaning etch. **Intervention:** Explicitly teach 'focus' using a range of short activities such as copying a picture or logo. Increase the duration of time spent on preferred tasks to develop attention span. Vary activities building in sensory or movement breaks.	**Adjustment:** Adults use questions to encourage the learner to identify what information they have and to recall prior experience that may help them. **Support:** Learner works with peer buddy or adult who may provide clues or additional information including structured choices to aid thinking. Use worksheets or photos to aid recall. **Intervention:** Explicitly teach problem solving by rehearsing hypothetical situations or scenarios that require resolution. Play games or treasure hunt type puzzles that structure information and encourage the identification of next steps.
Making Things	**Motivation**
Adjustment: The adults seek to integrate creativity into teaching and share how they make things, promoting a culture of exploration. Vary the modality of learning, so learners can use a range of stimuli. **Support:** Provide opportunities for collaborative projects in pairs or small groups. Use kits or models that provide skill rehearsal and scaffold actions into smaller steps. **Intervention:** Explicitly teach skills and techniques such as cutting, measuring and connecting materials and rehearse their application. Explicitly teach how to follow instructions or recipes.	**Adjustment:** Adults can praise and encourage, providing positive feedback and sharing success with others. Develop a whole class positive rewards programme as a motivator. **Support:** Establish a clear now and next structure so the learner receives a reward or a preferred activity following engagement. Personalise rewards so they have direct meaning for the learner. **Intervention:** Use coaching techniques to encourage the learner to set goals and next steps. Promote the visualisation of achievement and success and link these to positive feelings.
Trust	**Courage – Determination**
Adjustment: Adults should remain consistent fair and predictable in interactions with learners, projecting trust and positive belief in all. **Support:** Use visual reminders such as class agreements or codes of conduct to remind learners or expectations. Refer to prior positive experiences and label feelings and emotions. **Intervention:** Explore the meaning of trust working with the learner individually or in a small group. Share social scenarios or stories that illustrate times of trust and feelings of disappointment, encourage the learner to relate to themselves.	**Adjustment:** Adults create a culture of 'having a go' and label actions that show courage and determination. **Support:** Build in an expectation of mistakes by introducing "5 lives" or attempts, so the learner does not become despondent. Praise and model sustained effort and celebrate achievements. **Intervention:** Use coaching techniques to identify goals and aspirations and the actions that are necessary for achievement. Explicitly describe feelings of bravery and link these to stories or scenarios to aid understanding. Provide a range of new experiences and label the learners positive responses to these.

The 7 Cs Action Cards

Control

Control	**Self-regulation**
Behaviour for Learning	**Anxiety Management**
Confidence	**Resilience**
Language of Emotions	**Independence**

The 7 Cs Action Cards

Control – Adjustment, Support & Intervention Ideas

Self-regulation **Adjustment:** Adult remains vigilant and anticipates 'warning' signs or triggers. Applies positive redirection or calm reminder of action to take, e.g. time out engaging with preferred activity. **Support:** Creation of 'safe' space for learner to retreat to. Access to 'calm' box of soothing toys or resources chosen by learner for use when losing regulation. **Intervention:** Explicit teaching of language of emotions and actions associated with each feeling. Sign posting to individual triggers and indicators of distress combined with positive calming actions. Teach mindfulness techniques for learner to try.	**Control**
Anxiety Management **Adjustment:** Adult anticipates potential triggers and provides advanced warning and preparation. Remain calm and reassure safety. Use questions as reminder of own strategies **Support:** Access to comforters, e.g. preferred toy, book, music or tablet for distraction. Personalised calming box of resources and access to safe place. **Intervention:** Explicitly teach CBT techniques such as thinking bias and automatic negative thoughts and encourage learner to consider likelihood of occurrence. Rehearse actions to take when anxiety increases.	**Behaviour for Learning** **Adjustment:** Adult provides explicit description of positive behaviours for learning and explains their relevance. Praise learners adopting the behaviours. Reduce distractions and consider the learners proximity to the adult. **Support:** Learner has access to a work-station for specific tasks. Access to headphones to screen out distractions, adult reminds and positively reinforces attention and focus. **Intervention:** Explicitly teach listening and attention skills, where appropriate, teach note taking and or mind mapping. Rehearse independent skills and using a resource checklist.
Resilience **Adjustment:** Adults model perseverance by demonstrating uncertainty and sustained effort. They create a culture of "try and try again" rewarding effort and learning associated with effort. **Support:** Time to work with peers and or an adult engaging in activities that will lead to success and enjoyment. Promote opportunity for learner to apply strengths and to talk about skills. **Intervention:** In pairs or small groups, adult explores feelings and behaviour that promote resiliency. Learners engage in 'difficult' tasks collaboratively, sharing strategies and next steps. Teach language of resiliency and belief.	**Confidence** **Adjustment:** Adult models the use of positive 'I can' statements and projects belief in capacity of learners. Use questions to encourage learner to identify strengths and success. **Support:** Provide resources that learner associates with success of feeling valued, e.g. work with class mascot/ toy or use 'special' pen. Work in groups with positively assigned roles. **Intervention:** Explicitly 'teach' confidence to the learner by focusing on occasions when they have felt confident. Use stories to help define what confidence looks and feels like. Encourage learner to 'notice' such times and record in diary/voice recorder.
Independence **Adjustment:** Adults use questions to encourage learner to 'self-solve' issues or uncertainties. Ensure tasks are differentiated and accessible for all. **Support:** Adult may mediate learning by asking questions and providing prompts to scaffold participation. Adult does not sit next to the learner, but offers support, moves away, then returns. **Intervention:** Explicitly teach learning routines and provide independent prompt sheets and checklists for learner. Teach strategies or questions the learner can ask of themselves to complete tasks. Identify prior success and strengths.	**Language of Emotions** **Adjustment:** Adults integrate language of emotions within interactions and use rating scales to express their own feelings. **Support:** Use of visual images or cards to help learner track feelings during a day. Record feelings in a diary or book. **Intervention:** Explicitly teach language of emotions and encourage learner to identify events or actions that have triggered feelings. Alternatively use stories to illustrate feelings and describe how people look and act when they feel a certain way. Encourage learner to identify images and the feelings they present.

The 7 Cs Action Cards

Compassion

Compassion	**Friendships**
Turn-taking	**Empathy**
Sense of Justice	**Self-esteem & Wellbeing**
Self-efficacy	**Support for Others**

The 7 Cs Action Cards

Compassion – Adjustment, Support & Intervention Ideas

Friendships	Compassion
Adjustment: Adult provides opportunities for learner to work with peers and seeks to 'broker' friendship via shared experiences. **Support:** Adult teaches structured games to learner and small group or peers to facilitate structured interaction at unstructured times. Set up 'friendship bench' or interest club for peers. **Intervention:** Explicitly teach how to initiate interaction and rehearse 'ice breakers.' Consider setting up a 'circle of friends' to look out for the learner during break and lunch times.	

Empathy	Turn-taking
Adjustment: Adult integrates examples of empathy by labelling 'possible' feelings of others when reading stories or in conversation with learners. **Support:** Adult may need to intervene in discussions or interactions to pose questions to explain impact of actions on feelings. Adult can signpost feelings using emoji cards. **Intervention:** Explicitly teach a range of emotions and feelings and discuss the presentation of these in ourselves and others. Rehearse skills by looking at photos, stories or film clips and use emoji cards to select feelings.	**Adjustment:** Adult models the phrase of 'my turn, your turn' when discussing or interacting with learners. Adult facilitates opportunities for structured games or interaction. **Support:** Learner works with peer buddy or adult to rehearse turn-taking when playing games. Use physical resource such as tapping a bell to indicate my turn your turn. **Intervention:** Adult explicitly teaches 'my turn, your turn' and rehearses skill regularly by engaging with a variety of games or activities.

Self-esteem & Wellbeing	Sense of Justice
Adjustment: Adults model the use of positive language and praise and create a culture of recognition and compliments. Adults ask learners to identify what they think they have done well and why this is useful. **Support:** Specific and structured questions are asked of a learner to encourage reflection on success and strengths. They choose from examples what they think is successful **Intervention:** In pairs or small groups, learners explore an 'about me' activity where they identify strengths, positive attributes and successes. Coaching techniques can be used.	**Adjustment:** Adult establishes and refers to a consistent and 'fair' classroom culture with clear expectations regarding interactions and an agreed code of conduct. **Support:** Use structured dialogue to understand conflict and to provide guidance for resolution. Establish peer supporters or provide adult time to listen to accounts or concerns. **Intervention:** Explicitly teach tools for managing and resolving conflict and frustrations including 'restorative' type approaches. Rehearse the application of these using role play based on stories or social scenarios, promoting fairness.

Support for Others	Self-efficacy
Adjustment: Adults provide opportunities for learner to work or play alongside supportive peers. Label positive support shown by peers defining why this was supportive. **Support:** Teach team or paired games and promote collaborative and supportive interaction. Model support and praise and ask learner to 'notice' support from others. **Intervention:** Explicitly teach when an action or behaviour is supportive and helpful or destructive and negative. Discuss associated feelings and rehearse 'scripts' or conversation starters that could promote positive interactions and support for others.	**Adjustment:** Adults promote individual efficacy by asking learners to choose resources and equipment to use for tasks and using structured choices help the learner to make decisions. **Support:** Adults encourage learners to share ideas and information and feedback to class or small group. Learner selects and leads others in an activity or game. **Intervention:** Explicitly demonstrate learner's independence and impact by enabling play or self-directed learning. Structure questioning to support development of idea but ensure that ownership is with the learner who can self-determine actions.

<u>The 7 Cs Action Cards</u>

<u>Co-ordination</u>

Co-ordination	**Fine Motor Skills**
Gross Motor Skills	**Sensory**
Mobility	**Stability & Balance**
Posture	**Sensory Processing**

The 7 Cs Action Cards

Co-ordination – Adjustment, Support & Intervention Ideas

Fine Motor Skills **Adjustment:** Adult ensures access to alternative means of recording or adjusts recording requirements so learner can work within a pair or small group. **Support:** Learner has access to a variety of aids or adapted equipment including pencil grips, writing slopes, laptop, voice recorder. **Intervention:** Individual programme to rehearse fine motor skills including vertical, horizontal and circular mark making in isolation and activities to develop fluency and control of distal muscles, e.g. cutting, threading, pinching, colouring, weaving etc.	**Co-ordination**
Sensory **Adjustment:** Adult may adapt mode of communication to overcome sensory barriers, e.g. use of microphone & hearing loop. **Support:** Access to auxiliary aids as deemed appropriate. Adult may attempt to overcome barriers by describing or using alternative means of communication, e.g. Braille or sign. **Intervention:** Explicitly teach other means of communication where sensory barriers exist. Promote and refine other sensory experiences.	**Gross Motor Skills** **Adjustment:** Adult ensures accessible physical environment and uses equipment or aids to enable participation. **Support:** Learner has access to adapted equipment which enables engagement. Learner may require physical support to complete certain tasks or movements. **Intervention:** Explicit teaching and rehearsal of individual skills as required. Learner may need to follow an individualised programme to develop fluency and accuracy with jumping, hopping, running, walking, throwing, catching or kicking a ball.
Stability & Balance **Adjustment:** The adult ensures equality of access to learning tasks by adapting materials or requirements as necessary. **Support:** Specific and personalised aids as required such as, standing frames, supportive cushions, sloping desks etc. **Intervention:** Implement an individualised learning programme as suggested by a physio or occupational therapist. Liaise with learner and their family to identify key activities for rehearsal.	**Mobility** **Adjustment:** Adult regularly reviews tasks to ensure that no learner is disadvantaged or prohibited from participation due to the mobility demands of a task. Adjust outcome or expression. **Support:** Promote the independent use of aids or equipment that enable movement and engagement. Rehearse use and ensure access barriers are overcome. **Intervention:** Where appropriate, implement an individualised physio or occupational therapy programme to develop movement and mobility.
Sensory Processing **Adjustment:** Adult audits sensory environment considering sensory demands on leaner, making changes or adaptions where necessary. **Support:** Introduce equipment to help filter sensory information such as headphones and sunglasses to help screen out sounds and sights. **Intervention:** Explicitly rehearse sensory skills so learner gains more experience processing information, such as blowing bubbles, chewing, singing, tracking lights. Where appropriate implement an individualised programme.	**Posture** **Adjustment:** Adult adapts environment to accommodate range of working positions, including sitting at desk, standing at desk, laying on floor or cushion. **Support:** Integrate regular breaks and provide opportunities for movement between tasks. Audit seat height and provide foot guide or seated cushions to promote effective posture. **Intervention:** Rehearse core muscle exercises following an individualised programme. Audit preferred seating positions and promote fluency of transitioning between spaces.

The 7 Cs Action Cards

Curriculum

Curriculum	**English**
Maths	**Science**
Art & Music	**History & Geography**
Computing	**PE & Sport**

The 7 Cs Action Cards

Curriculum – Adjustment, Support & Intervention Ideas

English	Curriculum
Adjustment: Adapt the task to overcome barriers to learning such as reading, writing or spelling, providing alternative means of expression or recording. **Support:** Provide key word sheets, sentence starters, letter prompts and word builders. Encourage learner to use a laptop with read aloud text or a reader pen or voice recorder. **Intervention:** Explicitly teach rules and strategies for reading, writing and spelling. Baseline skills and target next steps using direct instruction, interleaved learning and provide short but regular opportunities for rehearsal.	

Science	Maths
Adjustment: Adult ensures availability of visual prompts or modelled examples of concepts. They integrate key vocabulary and check out the learner's understanding at the start of a task. **Support:** Provide vocabulary or equipment lists relevant to the topic and structured recording forms. Promote peer collaboration/discussion, ensuring positive role models in each group. **Intervention:** Explicitly teach and rehearse key concepts and vocabulary, defining the relevance and links between topics.	**Adjustment:** Adult interleaves prior learning to prompt and remind learner of relevant rules and procedures. **Support:** Learner works with peer buddy or adult who can prompt, remind or scaffold information. Provide access to visual resources and aids. **Intervention:** Explicitly audit existing skills and target rehearsal of gaps or uncertainties. Provide regular opportunities for revision and use reference books or sheets to aid independent recall of information. Make explicit the implicit regarding the purpose and application of key concepts.

History & Geography	Art & Music
Adjustment: The adult adapts materials and content to ensure access for all learners. The relevance and potential application of information is made explicit to all learners. **Support:** Learners have an opportunity to work with peers or in groups with an adult to explore information in more detail. Questions are used alongside prompts or artefacts to promote thinking and encourage motivation. **Intervention:** The adult explicitly teaches key concepts as pre-teaching to enable access and scaffold understanding. Concepts and vocabulary are personalised for the learner.	**Adjustment:** Adults promote a culture of exploration and encourage effort. Equipment is available for independent rehearsal and adult integrates skills into teaching. **Support:** Equipment is adapted where necessary to promote access. Skills may be isolated for structured rehearsal and additional resources or examples are shared with learners. **Intervention:** Isolated skills are explicitly taught and regularly rehearsed by the learner. Individually or in small groups, prior examples are shared and discussed with opportunities for personalised replication.

PE & Sport	Computing
Adjustment: Adults adjust expectations, rules or activity content to accommodate individual needs, setting personalised targets or a range of related tasks. **Support:** Adapted or modified equipment may be available to learners, to aid access to the activity. Skills may be isolated and their application scaffolded for rehearsal. **Intervention:** Explicitly teach methods and skills to develop greater efficiency, fluency and accuracy. Watch professional games and identify skills applied and set personal goals for improvement.	**Adjustment:** Adults integrate IT into all aspects of learning and model the efficiency and potential of devices. Learners can use equipment as a chosen method for expressing their work. **Support:** Adult or peer supporters provide visual or verbal guidance to aid independent use of equipment. Film clips or presentations are available as prompts. **Intervention:** Explicitly pre-teach skills, vocabulary and the method of using equipment so the learner is able to rehearse and apply skills of application.

The deployment of teaching assistants (TAs)

Nowhere is the need for clarity of purpose and intent greater, than in relation to the deployment of adults to support learning. The use of teaching assistants (TAs) or learning support assistants (LSAs) is a well-versed topic amongst SENCOs and SEN Practitioners. Yet it remains highly contentious for some. Historically, the origins of additional adults evolved with clear intent. As the name suggests, many additional adults were initially employed to assist teachers, be that with the preparation of resources, the presentation of work (i.e., wall displays) or to be an extra pair of hands, eyes and ears as class sizes grew. But as the identification of SEN increased, so the potential grew for additional adults to 'help' learners with SEN. The trend for employing support staff increased until a significant percentage of the school workforce were and indeed are TAs, and their tasks have become more specialist and individual pupil-led. In some situations, this resulted in a number of additional adults being placed in the same classrooms at the same time, to support individual learners. But despite the ever-increasing adult to child ratio (which in theory could have spread support across the class), the remit and responsibilities for some adults became narrower and individually focused. This fuelled the risk that some learners with SEND were never alone or able to work directly with peers, as they had 1:1 support and 'their' TA was by their side at all times. **Research began to notice that instead of enhancing learning and independence, this 'Velcro' model of support, isolated learners from peers and teachers. It also limited their opportunity to make mistakes and therefore to learn *from* mistakes. Instead, this model created over dependency and at times resulted in the creation of passive learners displaying signs of learned helplessness.** Of course, the motives of the adults working with the learners were well-placed and generally originated from a desire to help, support and to do their job effectively. Afterall, if they were employed as a 1:1 they sought to deliver 1:1 support. There is no fault or criticism at the individual adult for that. But there is a case for the critical evaluation of this system and the adult 'helper' culture that it created.

Such critical evaluation is evidenced in various sources, including Ofsted and a significant research project into the effective deployment of TAs, the Deployment and Impact of Support Staff (DISS) project, which was a longitudinal study that took place between 2003 and 2008. It investigated the impact of TAs on teachers, teaching and pupils' learning, behaviour and academic progress.

Although the findings suggested that TAs and other support staff had a positive effect on teachers' workload, job satisfaction and stress, it also found little evidence that TAs had a positive effect on learning or outcomes. Indeed, the DISS project findings challenged the assumption that TAs enhance academic progress of learners. It also noted that those learners working with TAs had less contact with teachers and were potentially missing out from input from teachers. The report findings are detailed within the book *Reassessing the Impact of Teaching Assistants* by Blatchford, Russell and Webster (2012.) A year later, in 2013, the authors wrote a further book *Maximising the Impact of Teaching Assistants*, which provided guidance for school leaders and teachers on the recommendations of the DISS project.

The DISS project and emerging views of the time, implied that the deployment of TAs to individual learners was counter-productive for learning. It also raised the concern that those who find learning the most difficult (i.e., learners with SEN) were frequently being taught by TAs rather than qualified teachers. Furthermore, it was noted that often, these learners had significantly less time with teachers compared to learners without SEN. Other research also questioned the impact of time spent with TAs on learning outcomes, indeed the Education Endowment Foundation now describe TAs as a high-cost provision with relatively low impact. On their Teaching and Learning Toolkit, they state: "Teaching Assistants – low impact for high costs based on limited evidence."

The publication of this research was closely followed by a sustained period of financial austerity which significantly impacted on school budgets. For many, this resulted in redundancy or restructuring, which has significantly reduced the numbers of TAs available in schools and settings. Although the overall conclusions of the DISS project were negative with regards to the impact of TAs on learning, they did attribute this to the way in which schools and teachers deployed and prepared TAs for their role. **Indeed, my experience and observations have shown that targeted additional adult time can be highly effective to learning. If the adult is trained and has an explicit and relevant purpose, then their support can be invaluable to overcoming or removing barriers to learning.** The Education Endowment Foundation have produced a useful summary, *Making Best Use of Teaching Assistants*. Within this they identify seven key elements, including ensuring that TAs are not used as an informal teaching resource for low attaining pupils. Second, that TAs should be used to add value to what teachers do and not as a replacement to the teacher. Third, TAs should be used to help pupils develop independent learning skills to manage their own learning. The fourth recommendation is that schools should also ensure that TAs are fully prepared for their role in the classroom. The fifth suggestion is that TAs can be used to deliver high- quality one-to-one and small group support using structured interventions. The school should adopt evidence-based interventions to support TAs and, finally, to ensure that there is an explicit connection between all sources of teaching and learning.

Implications for SENCOs and SEN Practitioners

 The implication of this is not, therefore, to eradicate the role of TAs or to disregard their contribution, but to move away from a culture where TAs are perceived to be 'helping' learners, to a culture where TAs are trained and skilled to facilitate targeted support *for* learning, commissioned by teachers. This requires clear expectations regarding the anticipated impact of such support as well as training and development for staff delivering the support and those who are commissioning the support (i.e., teachers.) Clarity of purpose regarding the anticipated and actual impact of support for learning is essential. And it is this that led to the development of 'the 4 Functions of Learning Support' model to be explored in the next chapter.

Reflections

• Are your teachers 'commissioners' of TA time, providing clarity of purpose regarding action and anticipated impact of the action?
• Are your TAs trained and supported to fulfil their roles, maximising the impact on learning?
• If your TAs are working with learners with SEND, are they trained to use evidence-based interventions and promote independence?

References

The Education Endowment Foundation Teaching and Learning Toolkit (2020) Available at https://educationendowmentfoundation.org.uk/ (Accessed 1 May 2021)

Making Best Use of Teaching Assistants (2018) The Education Endowment Foundation. Available at https://educationendowmentfoundation.org.uk/ (Accessed 1 May 2021).

Maximising the Impact of Teaching Assistants (2013) Peter Blatchford, Anthony Russell and Rob Webster. Abingdon: Routledge.

Reassessing the Impact of Teaching Assistants (2012) Peter Blatchford, Anthony Russell and Rob Webster. Abingdon: Routledge.

Special Educational Needs and Disability Code of Practice: 0 to 25 years – Statutory Guidance for Organisations which Work with and Support Children and Young People who have Special Educational Needs or Disabilities (2014; updated 2015). Department for Education and Department of Health.

4. The 4 Functions of Learning Support

The 4 Functions of Learning Support is a framework that was written to facilitate a shared language of support between teachers and TAs. It arose from the observation that when asked, TAs would frequently describe their work with children as "helping". Similarly, when teachers were asked what TAs were doing with a group, they too would say "helping". Although the word 'helping' aptly describes the intent of the behaviour, it is difficult to measure the effectiveness or impact of 'helping', or when helping should start and finish. **The 4 Functions model *defines* support for learning. It describes what learning support actually looks like, which enables informed direction and commissioning, which in turn allows impact to be measured.** So, what are the 4 Functions of Learning Support?

The 4 Functions model states that TAs will either be providing **MEDIATION**, **REINFORCEMENT** of a skill or learning behaviour, carrying out an **ASSESSMENT** or delivering an **INTERVENTION**. The introduction of this language can give TAs clarity of focus regarding expectations of their work and empower teachers to commission or request action with a specific purpose. It also means that SENCOs and or SEN Practitioners can account for the deployment of TA time and capture how much time is spent on each activity, as well as demonstrating the impact of this time.

Function 1: Mediation

Mediation is the process of facilitating learning. It is influenced by Vygotsky's Zone of Proximal Development, a theory which describes the position where a person moves from what they know, to learning something new. The zone is the space between not knowing something and knowing it. I think of it as the transitional stage, where you 'sort of' know what is being said but not quite! I know when I am in my own zone of proximal development because I usually start to get a headache and plead with the person to say a bit more as I 'nearly' understand. In real terms for us in schools and settings, it is the 'goosebump' moment. It is that point where you can actually 'see' learning taking place. For me, there is nothing more rewarding than when the learner then proceeds through the zone of proximal

DOI: 10.4324/9781003179436-4

development and they, and you, realise that they understand it! Mediation is the facilitation of this process.

Mediation involves asking questions of a learner, rather than giving them answers. Many adults (myself included) give too much information to learners. We are motivated by the desire to help or to explain but end up demonstrating our *own* prior learning rather than facilitating new learning for that learner. How many times have you observed, either in yourself or others, the one-sided conversation? It begins with an instruction such as,

> "Ok Joe let's get started, here's your book, where is your pencil? Find your pencil as you need to write the date and then start writing your story... here's your pencil, now write the date on this line, you know we always write the date here... the date is on the board Joe... let me write it here."

Does that sound familiar? I admit that for the benefit of this example, it is slightly exaggerated, but I have genuinely observed similar conversations. This is presented here not to criticise or belittle adults working with children, quite the contrary. This colleague is only 'guilty' of wanting to support Joe to get on with his work. Yet with support, training and guidance on how to *mediate* learning, the interaction could be very different. For example,

> "Joe, what have you been asked to do? Yes, that's right, you are writing a story about your holiday. What will you need to start writing? Yes, your book and ...? Excellent, now you have your book and pencil, what do you have to write every lesson, so you can remember when you were doing this work? That's right, the date. Where is the date written every day? Excellent, I will let you get started and will come back to read your opening sentence."

The use of questions to help learners to focus on learning is an incredibly powerful approach. We often deploy adults to work with groups of learners, to *help* scaffold their access to the differentiated learning task. **Commissioning adults to *mediate* learning with a group, is far more empowering, as it is clear that they are *facilitating the learning process,* rather than helping the learner to complete a task.** Mediation is also measurable. For example, if the TA is mediating learning with a group of six learners, and six out of six were able to access the task, then the mediator can demonstrate impact. Shifting the focus and language of learning support to mediation rather than 'helping' is also useful as it will reveal the appropriateness or, at times, the inappropriateness of a differentiated task. **The quality of differentiation in a school or setting is essential knowledge for SENCOs and SEN Practitioners. Additional adults cannot be used to 'compensate' for ineffective teaching or differentiation.** Mediation is about scaffolding access to a task, it is not about replanning the entire lesson because the set task is inaccessible. If TAs do find themselves in a position where they are in effect planning the teaching for an individual or group of learners, this needs to be discussed with the teacher and the SENCO or SEN Practitioner. I have witnessed incredibly skilled TAs do exactly this and do it really well. But however insightful their planning and delivery maybe, the teacher is still responsible for teaching all learners. The TA may have the required knowledge of the learner, but they are not necessarily trained or paid enough to carry out this responsibility. Of course, excellent teachers work with all those who know the learner the best, so should be working in collaboration with the TA and indeed the parent or carer and the learner themselves, but ultimately the planning and implementation of learning opportunities is the responsibility of the class and/or subject teacher. **Mediation does not compensate for inadequate teaching, but it does complement effective teaching.**

Function 2: Reinforcement of a skill or learning behaviour

The second of the 4 Functions of Learning Support, is reinforcement. In real terms, this is where the adult seeks to remind the learner of a particular skill or learning behaviour whilst promoting independence. In many ways this is often the unspoken role of the TA. They will remind learners to use capital letters or full stops, to write the date, to face the front when listening and to put the pencil down when everyone has been asked to stop and listen. In fact, this sort of reminding provides an essential service and function for many learners. It can also be the comment that provides gentle encouragement, explicit praise, or a quiet whispered 'warning' which again, helps to focus and redirect many learners. However, to capture this essential role without the language of 'reinforcement' is hard. This sort of interaction can be perceived as vague, soft, or even parental and may not therefore be valued or considered essential. Yet, by describing the action as the *reinforcement of a skill or a learning behaviour*, it is immediately transformed into an explicit and accountable action. **Teachers can use the language of the 4 Functions of Learning Support to specifically request action for an**

individual or group of learners. The TA is also clear of the expectations regarding their engagement in that lesson. And both the teacher and TA have a shared construct or language of intent. So, if asked by a governor, Ofsted or member of the Senior Leadership Team, what the TA is doing, they would both respond by saying, "In this lesson they are reinforcing the skill of capital letters and full stops with two groups." Furthermore, because of the explicit intent of action, its success and impact can be measured. For example, if the TA is reinforcing the skill of capital letters and full stops, at the end of the session, the teacher can count how many of the group(s) did use capital letters and full stops, which would illustrate the effectiveness of this reinforcement. Of course, this level of scrutiny and accountability is not required on a lesson-by-lesson basis, but it does lend itself to monitoring at specific time intervals.

Function 3: Assessment

Gathering assessment information is the third of our 4 Functions of Learning Support. TAs could be deployed to complete observations of a learner or a group of learners. This may be a verbatim-style observation where they record what is seen, or it could be that they are asked to complete a focused observation which seeks to record a particular behaviour or action. Similarly, it may be a timed interval observation, where a snapshot description of behaviour is recorded every ten minutes. Of course, to maximise the potential of such information gathering, TAs will need to be trained and expectations made explicit, but the potential benefit from such regular information gathering for the SENCO or SEN Practitioner is huge.

Assessment could also be in the form of completing and updating a particular skill baseline or progress measure. This could include ascertaining the number of sounds accurately identified before and after an intervention, or it could be facilitating a curriculum subject skills review. Additional adults can also be used highly effectively to gather information from learners themselves. They could meet with learners before an intervention, asking questions about their confidence and hopes or expectations of the intervention. The use of rating scales can be extremely useful to aid such a process. Similarly, TAs could be asked to elicit the views of parents or carers at different points in the year, by phoning to ask three simple questions that relate to parental confidence or satisfaction regarding provision received by their child. The assessment options are vast, but do of course require explicit training, clarity of purpose and clear commissioning, from either the teacher, SENCO or SEN Practitioner.

Function 4: Intervention

Delivering an intervention with an individual or group of learners is the fourth and final of our 4 Functions of Learning Support. Here, the TA is asked to work with an individual or a small group either in the classroom or outside of the room, to engage with a particular intervention. The intervention should have been selected and commissioned by the class or subject teacher, in consultation with the SENCO or SEN Practitioner, with the intent of improving a particular skill. There are various published interventions which TAs are actively involved in delivering, but there is also the potential for developing in-school or Trust-type interventions. The key requirement of both of the approaches is to ensure that the TA has been sufficiently trained in the delivery of the intervention and feels confident and competent to deliver this. **Too often, TAs are given a 'pack' and asked to share the activity with a group. This is not facilitating an intervention. At best this is the promotion of a shared learning experience. At worst, it is a missed opportunity which sets both the TA and the learners up to fail. Facilitating an intervention is a skill that requires training and support. Our TAs are well- placed to achieve this, but only with relevant training and ongoing support.**

The resources that follow offer a starting-point for your consideration.

The 4 Functions of Learning Support

A Framework for the Deployment of Teaching Assistant Time

Teaching Assistants (TAs) account for around a quarter (28%) of the overall state-funded school workforce in England according to the DfE (2018.) There has been both praise and criticism about the impact of TAs on learning, but an emerging consensus suggests that positive impact links to evidence of a concise, complementary role of TAs to teachers (not a replacement). TAs must also be professionally trained and supported to fulfil a defined role.

Defining the specific purpose of TA deployment is not always clear or consistent. Colleagues may describe their work as "helping" children with their learning with teachers adopting the same descriptor. Although anyone working in education will have an insight into what "helping" could look like, it is far from measurable and its impact can be vague. Agreeing a 'language' of learning support can help to define outcomes and thus measure impact. The 4 Functions of Learning Support is one such framework.

In order to account for the distribution and impact of Teaching Assistant (TA) time, the purpose of allocation must be explicit and shared by teacher and TA. The 4 Functions model identifies four possible functions or actions. These can be used to determine the targeted purpose of TA time as well as a means of moderating impact. Teachers and support staff using this shared language are able to account for targeted actions and demonstrate an explicit purpose of the deployment of the TA resource. The 4 Functions of Learning Support time are:

Mediation

Within a mediation role, the TA could be asked to 'scaffold' access to class teaching and to mediate between the differentiated task delivered by the teacher and the experience of the learner. This could be working with a small group or targeted individuals. They would ensure that the process is intentional, reciprocated, communicates meaning and has relevance so can be applied. The impact of the mediation function is measurable through the successful engagement with class or group tasks.

Reinforcement (of a skill or learning behaviour)

Within this function the TA could rehearse a skill with a learner as part of their preparation for a new task or remind them of a skill or learning behaviour. This is also measurable through the successful participation of differentiated class-based tasks.

Assessment

Within the assessment function the TA may be asked to complete tasks, tests or observations of learners to inform the ongoing assessment of progress and needs. The information would be gathered for the teacher and/or SENCO or SEN Practitioner. The impact of assessment would be evidenced within teacher planning and timetabling of TA resources.

Intervention

Within this function the TA may be asked to deliver a targeted intervention programme intended to develop skill acquisition. This may be as part of a programme identified by an external agency, or as part of the support for learning package identified by the SENCO. The evidence for this would be within teacher planning and timetabling of TA resources.

Purpose

Introducing a shared framework of learning support, such as the 4 Functions model, promotes a common language for use by all staff. Teachers are enabled to become 'commissioners' of explicit and relevant SEN Support. Senior leaders are also able to monitor and account for deployment by sampling the distribution of TA time at regular intervals for example in the third week of a term, all staff are asked to simply complete a timetable indicating m, r, a or I, for timeslots. This information can be gathered to create the percentage of TA time spent in each role.

Overcoming Barriers to Learning	**Mediation**	**Reinforcement**	Overcoming Barriers to Learning
Attempting to Remove Barriers to Learning	**Assessment**	**Intervention**	Attempting to Remove Barriers to Learning

TA Timetable – Sampling Deployment Activities Example

Week Beginning:

Please complete the following timetable indicating the core function completed each session. Where 2 were applied, please indicate:

M = Mediation   R = Reinforcement of Skill or Learning Behaviour   A = Assessment   I = Intervention

Phase in Day	Monday	Tuesday	Wednesday	Thursday	Friday
Arrival	R	R	R	R	R
Lesson before break	M	A	M	A	M
Break	A	R	A	R	A
Lesson before lunch	M	I	M	I	M
Lunch	I	R	I	R	I
Lesson after lunch	I	R	I	R	I
Home time	R	R	R	R	R

TA Timetable – Sampling Deployment Activities

Week Beginning:

Please complete the following timetable indicating the core function completed each session. Where 2 were applied, please indicate:

M = Mediation   R = Reinforcement of Skill or Learning Behaviour   A = Assessment   I = Intervention

Phase in Day	Monday	Tuesday	Wednesday	Thursday	Friday
Arrival					
Lesson before break					
Break					
Lesson before lunch					
Lunch					
Lesson after lunch					
Home time					

Implications for SENCOs and SEN Practitioners

Excusing my obvious bias, but the potential implications for SENCOs and SEN Practitioners in the adoption of the 4 Functions of Learning Support are many and positive. Establishing this simple and concise shared language of learning support has the potential to empower teachers and TAs alike. The teacher is enabled to 'commission' learning support directly from the TA, and the TA (with appropriate training) is able to complete targeted actions (with intent) as requested by the teacher. This commissioning and delivery framework between the teacher and TA could result in their independence from the SENCO or SEN Practitioner, which enables your focus to shift on to quality assurance and the monitoring and capturing of impact of TA deployment. The resources provided in this chapter help to illustrate how such monitoring can occur. The important point to remember is that these activities would be completed at termly or six-monthly intervals, where you will be able to *sample* the deployment of TAs and examine their impact. This is not about you, teachers or TAs writing daily accounts of activities, but rather, your development of a system that 'tests' out the effectiveness of support for learning, at regular intervals.

The ultimate implication of the 4 Functions of Learning Support model for SENCOs and SEN Practitioners is the shift in perceived roles for teachers and TAs that this creates. Teachers become 'commissioners' of learning support, using a clear and shared language of learning support. Similarly, TAs become mediators, skill reinforcers, assessors or interventionists, instead of 'helpers', which in itself helps to redefine and shift the focus and purpose of engagement.

The 4 Functions Monitoring Form – Weekly Sample Autumn 2021 Example

Teacher as Commissioner

Teacher completes the focus section for each day, to be used and completed by the TA during the sample week.

Session		Monday	Tuesday	Wednesday	Thursday	Friday
1 Before break	Focus	Work with red group – mediate learning, promote independence and task completion	Work with blue & green group during literacy – reinforce problem solving via questioning	Intervention with 5 pupils – follow plan	Mediation with blue group – ensure independence and connections	Mediation with red and yellow group – monitor use of topic words
	Impact					
2 After break	Focus	Intervention work with 5 pupils group A – follow plan	Intervention work with 5 pupils group B – follow plan	Mediate red group – clarify understanding, monitor attention and task completion	Intervention work with 5 pupils group A – follow plan	Intervention with 5 pupils group B – follow plan
	Impact					
3 After lunch	Focus	Mediate for red and yellow group – focus on use of topic language	Assessment of yellow group progress with phonics	Assessment – mid-week learning mentor review of 3 children	Assessment of red group progress with phonics	Assessment – end of week learning mentor review
	Impact					

The 4 Functions Monitoring Form – Weekly Sample Autumn 2021 Example

Teacher as Commissioner

TA(s) complete the impact record on a daily basis during the sample week to feedback to the Teacher and SENCO or SEN Practitioner.

Session		Monday	Tuesday	Wednesday	Thursday	Friday
1 Before break	Focus	Work with red group – mediate learning, promote independence and task completion	Blue & green group during literacy – reinforce problem solving via questioning	Intervention with 5 pupils – follow plan	Mediation with blue group – ensure independence and connections	Mediation with red and yellow group – monitor use of topic words
	Impact	4 out of 6 pupils completed task set. JP and GM did not understand sequencing of sentence; required support	Blues got on well, no problems. JC, SA and LC distracted not complete task	4/5 attended, MR absent. Plan completed	6/6 pupils on task, independent and very enthusiastic about project	Red used word bank independently, JP needed prompting. Yellows completed but some silly comments
2 After break	Focus	Intervention work with 5 pupils group A – follow plan	Intervention work with 5 pupils group B – follow plan	Mediate red group – clarify understanding, monitor attention and task completion	Intervention work with 5 pupils group A – follow plan	Intervention with 5 pupils group B – follow plan
	Impact	MR was absent, but all other pupils completed session, see plan	All 5 attended session according to plan. JP quiet and distracted	Red group completed task. JP was distracting, but did get on with prompting.	5/5 attended, completed plan, MR needed to catch up from last session	All 5 attended, JP more engaged this session. Completed plan
3 After lunch	Focus	Mediate for red and yellow group – focus on use of topic language	Assessment of yellow group progress with phonics	Assessment – mid-week learning mentor review of 3 children	Assessment of red group progress with phonics	Assessment – end of week learning mentor review
	Impact	Lovely words used by red group, really grasped topic. Yellow needed more support, all ok apart from 2/6, JP and GM	Completed, although MR absent	JP acknowledged less focus this week. MR catching up since absence. Coached GM through sequencing	6/6 completed assessment, progress ranged from 3–8 new sounds – see individual record	6/6 felt positive about the week. JP commented on improvement in own learning behaviour as week went on. Agreed focus for next week

Teacher and SENCO/SEN Practitioner Analysis – Annual Summary following Sample Weeks Example

Sample Week	Deployment Focus: M, R, I, A	Evaluation of Impact
Autumn 1a	5/15 sessions mediation 1/15 sessions reinforcement 5/15 sessions intervention 4/15 sessions assessment	Effective deployment of TAs, used with clear focus and evidence of impact. 100% of sessions, delivered according to focus.
Autumn 1b	10/15 mediation 5/15 reinforcement 5/15 intervention 0/15 assessment	Good to see that mediation of all groups was shared between TA and class teacher. Positive account of progress. Sustained delivery of intervention sessions.
Spring 2a	5/15 mediation 5/15 reinforcement 0/15 intervention 5/15 assessment	Mediation appears to be working well. Greater use of assessment to help plan intervention choices.
Spring 2b	5/15 mediation 5/15 reinforcement 5/15 intervention 0/15 assessment	Greater use of in-class intervention. Useful way of introducing new skills and providing opportunity for rehearsal and preparation.
Summer 3a	6/15 mediation 4/15 reinforcement 1/15 intervention 4/15 assessment	Mediation remains dominant activity but balanced during this sample week.
Summer 3b	5/15 sessions mediation 5/15 sessions reinforcement 0/15 sessions intervention 5/15 sessions assessment	Assessment was used to gather information for the end of year reports. Mediation and reinforcement balanced equally. Few learners accessed interventions outside of class.

The 4 Functions Monitoring Form –
Weekly Sample Autumn

Teacher as Commissioner

Teacher completes the focus section for each day, to be used and completed by the TA during the sample week.
TA(s) complete the impact record on a daily basis during the sample week to feedback to the teacher and SENCO or SEN Practitioner.

Session		Monday	Tuesday	Wednesday	Thursday	Friday
1 Before break	Focus					
	Impact					
2 After break	Focus					
	Impact					
3 After lunch	Focus					
	Impact					

Teacher and SENCO/SEN Practitioner Analysis – Annual Summary following Sample Weeks

Sample Week	Deployment Focus: M, R, I, A	Evaluation of Impact
Autumn 1a		
Autumn 1b		
Spring 2a		
Spring 2b		
Summer 3a		
Summer 3b		

Reflections

- What is the current language of support for learning amongst teachers and TAs in your setting?
- Do your teachers currently perceive themselves as 'commissioners' of learning support?
- Could the 4 Functions of Learning Support provide a framework to aid your monitoring and quality assurance of TA deployment and impact?

5. Resources for mediation and reinforcement

Mediation and reinforcement are the first of the 4 Functions of Learning Support to be explored here. In many ways they represent the core work of TAs, as they are ultimately actions that intend to *overcome* the barriers to learning experienced by an individual or small group of learners. The adult working with the learner(s) will attempt to enable their access to, and completion of the set task. The adoption of the 4 Functions model is intended to empower teachers to specify or *commission* the support they require for that group or individual. If they deploy the TA to mediate access to the learning task, they are in fact requesting a different approach to when they deploy the TA to reinforce a skill or a learning behaviour. But what is this difference and what are the theoretical underpinnings of each approach?

Mediation

The term mediation, in this context, refers to a mediated learning experience as outlined by Feuerstein: "Mediation means any interaction in which an adult *intends* to convey a particular *meaning* or skill *and* encourages the child to *transcend*, that is, to relate the meaning to some other thought or experience" (Feuerstein and Lewin-Benham 2012, page 1).

A mediated learning experience involves three key partners, the *mediator* or adult who will intentionally seek to interact with the learner; the *stimulus*, which is the activity or resource to be explored; and the *mediatee* or learner themselves, who must be willing to engage, thus showing reciprocity to the mediator. **It is the interaction of the mediator and mediatee with the stimulus that has the potential to facilitate learning.** In their excellent book *Mediated Learning – Teaching, Tasks, and Tools to Unlock Cognitive Potential*, Mentis, Dunn-Bernstein and Mentis (2008) explore the essential elements of mediation, which Feuerstein argued transfers an adult–child interaction into a mediated learning experience. These

DOI: 10.4324/9781003179436-5

twelve criteria or types of interaction will be summarised here, as they represent the 'difference' between a TA 'helping' an individual or group of learners and a TA providing mediation. Of course, this is not to say that every TA, in every interaction with a learner, should or would be facilitating a mediated learning experience, but it is the existence of these criteria that provides the distinction between the commissioned function of mediation and reinforcement, or 'helping'.

Mentis et al. (2008) report that Feuerstein identified 12 criteria or types of interaction that are fundamental to mediation. He and they argue that the first three aspects are essential requirements of mediation. These are intentionality and reciprocity; meaning; and transcendence. **Intentionality & reciprocity** occurs when an action is deliberate and tries to guide towards a specific direction. Reciprocity occurs where there is an appropriate response from the mediatee or learner. Mentis et al. (2008) present a useful example of this in action, by referring to an occasion where someone puts out their hand to initiate the greeting of shaking hands (which demonstrates intentionality.) But the shaking of hands can only take place if the other person responds and connects their hand (demonstrating reciprocity.) In real terms this is a useful reminder that support for learning cannot be 'done' to a learner but can only be offered and reciprocated or refused by the learner. As teachers or TAs, we must never forget that we are 'offering' an action with the intent of advancing learning, but this can only be fulfilled if it is received and accepted by the learner. Ensuring that they understand what is on offer and why this might be important to them, relates to the second and third key components of mediation.

Mediation must involve clarity of **meaning**, which defines the purpose of the stimulus or activity. It is really useful to reflect on the perceived meaning that learners have of the tasks that we ask them to complete and even more so, the interventions or targeted tasks that we ask learners with SEND to engage with. One of my most revealing questions asked to learners following an observation, is 'what were you doing and why were you asked to do that?' If the response is generic such as 'to help me' this reveals a huge gap in shared perception of purpose or meaning. And whether you are a child or adult, if you don't know why you are doing something, you will certainly not be able to replicate it or use it in the future. This skill of application of learning is referred to by Feuerstein as **transcendence** and this is the third of the essential elements of mediation. It is described as the explicit attempt to promote future generalisation. 'This will be useful to me when ...'-type statements. It involves the summary or labelling of principles, concepts or strategies learnt in that session, to help learners connect when this could be used again. Mentis et al. (2008) state:

> Every single activity has in it the potential for transcendence. Transcendence is the bridge that connects related activities and ideas and links immediate needs to ever expanding needs.

> (page 30)

They go on to say:

> Consider the views of the cognitive psychologist Robert Sternberg who believed that an intelligent person is someone who is able to balance three kinds of skills: analytical skills (analysing and contrasting things,) creative skills (inventing and discovering things) and practical skills (applying skills in practice.) He called this the Triarchic Theory of Intelligence (Sternberg 1988) and said that intelligence involves balancing these three skills to suit the context or environment. Intelligent learning is not about remembering facts and information, but rather being able to analyse and evaluate information and think about it creatively, in order to apply it in different situations in ways that are appropriate for that situation.

> (page 33)

With regards to the 4 Functions of Learning Support and mediation in particular, the relevance is, I hope, obvious. **TAs as mediators, will promote active engagement with learners (ensuring intentionality and reciprocity), they will explain the purpose of the activity (providing meaning) and explain why this is useful, potentially summarising and labelling key learning points which will enable future application or transcendence. This is the function of mediation instead of simply reiterating or differentiating access to a learning task.** Alongside these three essential components of a mediated learning experience, Feuerstein, as described by Mentis et al. (2008), identifies nine additional attributes. These are:

- Competence
- Self-regulation and control of behaviour
- Sharing
- Individuation
- Goal planning

- Challenge
- Self-change
- Optimistic alternative
- Sense of belonging

In real terms, the mediator will balance each of these and integrate these principles where appropriate. For example, competence relates to developing the learner's self-confidence to have a go at the task. A learner who feels confident is likely to present with higher levels of motivation and self- efficacy (belief that they can effect change.) Mediation will include steps to empower learners to regulate their behaviour to give themselves the best possible chance for engagement and success. Mediation involves the principle of sharing, as the process itself promotes an interdependency between the mediator and mediatee. In this context, one cannot function without the other. They really are sharing in a learning experience. Individuation promotes a celebration of the uniqueness of every learner (and indeed mediator). It acknowledges and values difference, accepting that every adult and child has a unique combination of skills, interests and experiences that they bring to the learning context. Goal-setting is also a principle within mediation where the mediator may encourage and support the learner to set their own achievable goals. Similarly, the encouragement of a culture of challenge is a part of this process, where both the mediator and mediatee seek to challenge themselves, exploring their thinking and learning and demonstrating determination and enthusiasm for the process. The principle of self-change is essential to mediation, as it is part of the very foundation of this approach. It advocates a belief that learning is modifiable and therefore we all change and develop, and this is to be celebrated. It promotes a positive self- fulfilling prophecy, whereby the learner perceives themselves as having capacity to change and improve. Related to this is the principle of optimistic alternative, which simply requires that the mediator promotes a positive view to learning and challenges and seeks to identify solutions rather than dwell on problems or difficulties. This is highly relevant for our work with learners with SEND, as so often our 'language' and interaction become directed towards defining deficits, difficulties and barriers. The focus in mediation is on strengths, skills and solutions within the learner. Finally, the principle of a sense of belonging is promoted, which seeks to place the learner and learning within a context, where they can see themselves as contributors and participants. Mentis et al. (2008) state:

> With the right kind of scaffolding or mediation, learners can be challenged to learn today what they could not achieve yesterday. They can be supported

to attain what was previously just outside of their reach with the right kind of intervention. This relates well to Feuerstein's concept of intentionality and reciprocity, where with appropriate mediation (intentionality) a learner can be motivated to go that bit further than they are able to do if left to learn independently.

(page 17)

The concept of 'going that bit further', is also part of the rationale for adopting the 4 Functions of Learning Support. Providing a language of mediation, with explicit training and resources for TAs and teachers, will enable greater clarity for both the teacher as the commissioner of this approach and the TA as the 'commissioned'. The teacher is able to define the desired content or type of interaction that is required for an individual learner or a group and its anticipated impact. The resources in this chapter include a summary of the mediation process with defined principles, plus examples of mediated questions that TAs may use and adapt. There is also an inventory of resources or 'supplies' that TAs may want access to in order to mediate learning. This inventory is, as always, only offered as a starting point and contains a list of 'basic' equipment with a variety of applications. Your TAs will be able to add to this list, but if budgets allow, do create a physical 'support for learning' kit for your TAs, collating the equipment into a zip folder, so they have the resources to hand. And of course, rehearse the different ways of using the resources, so colleagues can feel confident in their role. We know from the Education Endowment Foundation's *Making Best Use of Teaching Assistants* recommendations that we should ensure that our TAs are fully prepared for their role in the classroom, which includes training and resources. The 4 Functions of Learning Support will also give your teachers and TAs a shared language to use to define deployment expectations and practice.

Questions to Support Mediation and Promote Learner Engagement

Questions that relate to getting started:

What do you need to do?

How could you make this happen?

Why is that a good idea?

Do you remember doing anything similar? What helped you?

Questions that promote reflection:

What do you have to do first?

Have you seen this before?

What is possible?

What do you think might happen if…?

Questions to aid focus:

What is your understanding?

What do you think?

What do you mean by that?

Am I right in thinking that…?

Questions that encourage more thinking:

Tell me more about that?

Is there anything else?

Why did you do that and not something else?

What do you expect to happen?

Questions to promote personal evaluation:

Do you like that?

Could it work for you?

Is that what you thought would happen?

What might happen next?

Questions that require more information:

Are there other options?

What about doing it a different way?

What would it look like?

Can you give me an example?

Questions that require generalisation:

How can this help you?

What have you learnt from this?

Will you use this again?

Can you share this with anyone?

Displaying active listening and building rapport

- Eye contact and open posture
- Paraphrase
- Mindfully listen
- Non-verbal signals
- Smile, mirror and match
- Empathy
- Tone of voice
- Common ground

Mediation Process Prompt

A Mediated Learning Experience must contain...

Intentionality	Reciprocity	Meaning	Transcendence
The learning activity must have a clear purpose and intent	The learning process is shared, the learner must want to engage	The activity must have a defined meaning and purpose for the learner	The learning should be relevant and be able to be applied in other contexts
This is what we are doing…	We are doing this together	This is why we are doing this…	This is how you can use this another time

Support for Learning – Practical Resources for Mediation

Ensure that those adults tasked with mediating learning with children or young people have immediate access to practical resources to aid them. Developing and distributing a Support for Learning Resource pack at the start of an academic year, ensures that Staff have the equipment they may need. Individuals will personalise resources, adding to the pack and sharing ideas with each other. As a starting point provide:

Item	Application(s)
Plastic zip wallet	• Storage of resources
Pens, pencils, rubber, sharpener	• 'Spare' recording tools
Spiral notebook	• To record observations or provide 'rough' working sheet for learner
Blue tack	• Instant visual 'counters' for those who do not want to be seen to use cubes but need a visual prompt • Fiddle 'toy' • Hold paper in position
Post-its – various sizes	• Spellings • Create jumbled sentences
Ruler	• Instant number line • Screen off words
Whiteboard & pen	• Create visual timetable or sequencing of activities • Encourage 'first' attempt
iPad	• Take photo of work instructions or working wall and place in front of student. • Voice-activated software • Siri support for spellings • Record teacher instructions for student to replay. • Create a film presentation of ideas • Type responses • Adult takes photos for assessment
Voice recorder	• Teacher records work instructions for Learner to play back • Learner records ideas for teacher to hear or for adult or peer to scribe
Plain white stickers	• Cover over 'mistakes' • Token reward system – each learner in group wears a sticker and a tally mark is drawn as a token reward which can be redited' for another reward later.
Reward stickers or commendation pass	• Praise and encouragement

Reinforcement of a skill or learning behaviour

The second of our 4 Functions of Learning Support also seeks to 'overcome' barriers to learning. Here the focus is on reminding or prompting learners. It is different to mediation in that the adult is not working directly with the learner as part of a shared experience. Instead, they may be monitoring, guiding, redirecting and refocusing as required. Depending on the age of the learners, this may be a role that is fulfilled across a whole class or a specified group (not necessarily just those with SEND or who are low- attaining), or indeed for an individual learner. The skill or learning behaviour that is to be reinforced should of course be made explicit to the learners involved. For younger children, reminding them that the TA is "looking for…" can be really powerful, indeed wearing a badge or lanyard with this focus drawn or written on, can be useful. For older learners, sharing the agreed focus and 'contracting' with them, whereby the TA agrees to 'notice' any discrepancies in their work or behaviour and discreetly point this out to them. The benefit of this is that it promotes learner ownership of the issue, and the TA is seen as a support to help *them* to develop their learning.

The resources for this function are less specific as they will of course be personal to each situation. That said there are templates for the "I'm looking for" sheets that maybe useful. For older learners, the use of post-it type reminders will be just as effective. The teacher should again be viewed as the 'commissioner' of this function and they would deploy adult support as deemed appropriate.

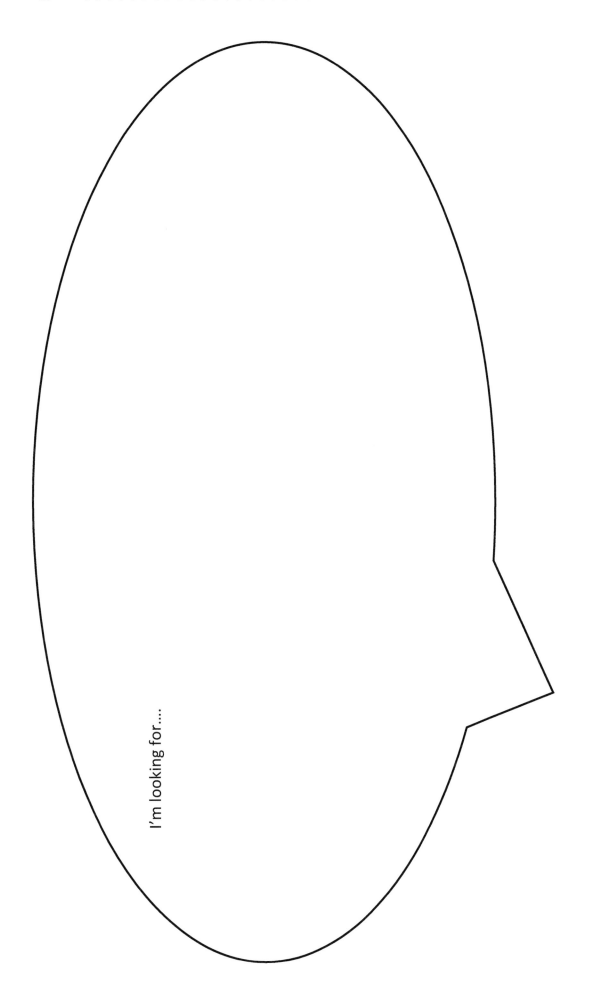

I'm looking for....

I'm thinking about...

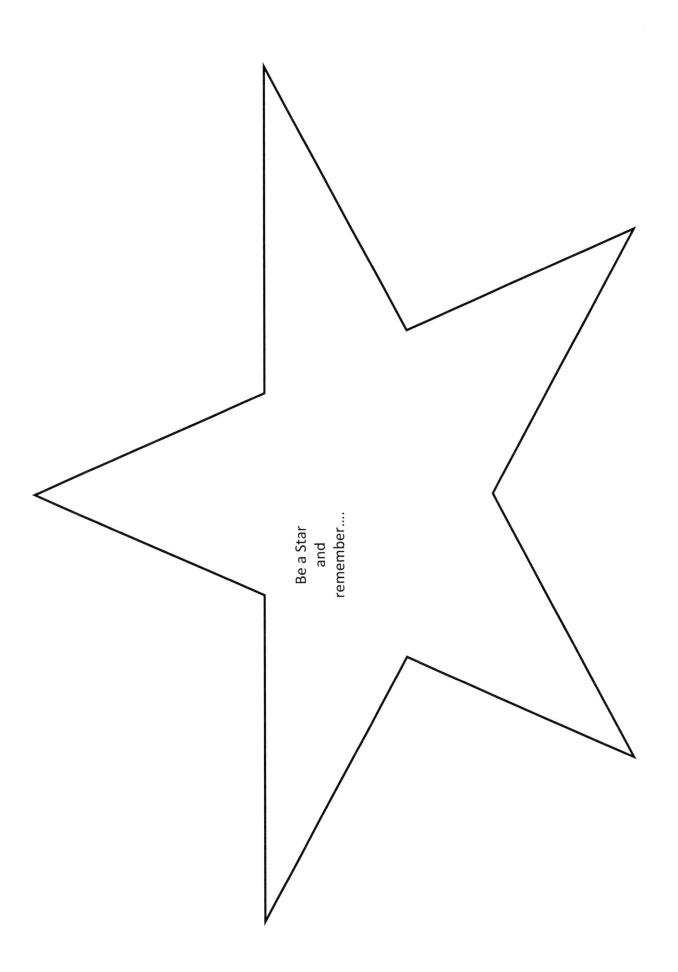

Be a Star
and
remember....

Implications for SENCOs and SEN Practitioners

The ultimate implication for SENCOs and SEN Practitioners is to consider whether the 4 Functions model could enhance the shared language of support for learning between teachers and TAs in your setting. If so, your next step is to share the approach and to develop training and resources, particularly on mediation. **Ensuring that teachers and TAs have a clear understanding of how mediation differs to helping, is the key. Emphasising the importance of intentionality, reciprocity, meaning and transcendence is an essential requirement to securing this development.** It is also at the heart of teaching and learning so should resonate with staff. Expanding the expectation that teachers are commissioners of learning support, via the deployment of resources and or TAs, is also key, which, again, is a positive and empowering approach, which has been welcomed by those staff who have adopted this framework. Take another look at the resources and see if they trigger your own thinking about transcendence and if they do, give it a go!

Reflections

- Do you like Feuerstein's principles of a mediated learning experience? Do they match your pedagogy and approach?
- How do TAs currently interact with learners in your school or setting? Are there systems in place for their training and development?
- Do you have a framework to capture how TAs are currently deployed and the quality and effectiveness of this learning exchange?

References

Making Best Use of Teaching Assistants (2018) The Education Endowment Foundation. Available at https://educationendowmentfoundation.org.uk/ (Accessed 1 May 2021).

Mediated Learning: Teaching, Tasks, and Tools to Unlock Cognitive Potential (2008) Mandia Mentis, Marilyn Dunn-Bernstein and Martene Mentis. Thousand Oaks, CA: Corwin.

The Triarchic Mind: A New Theory of Human Intelligence (1988) Robert J. Sternberg. New York: Viking.

What Learning Looks Like: Mediated Learning in Theory and Practice, K-6 (2012) Reuven Feuerstein and Ann Lewin-Benham. New York: Teachers College Press.

6. Resources for assessment and intervention

As with our previous chapter, our focus here will be upon the remaining of our 4 Functions of Learning Support. The functions of assessment and intervention tend to be targeted actions that seek to 'remove' barriers to learning (*if* the barrier has the potential to be removed). For example, if reading is a barrier to learning, then assessing the learner's starting point and providing a regular and targeted reading intervention, has the anticipated impact of teaching them to read and therefore *removing* that barrier. Commissioning TA time to complete these functions can be a useful approach for both the teacher, SENCO and SEN Practitioner. With appropriate training and support, the TA can gather information for the teacher, SENCO or SEN Practitioner, which can add to the rich picture of data about a learner. Let us begin with the assessment function.

Assessment

Assessment is fundamental to teaching and learning. As we discovered in our first book, *SEND Assessment: A Strengths-based Approach to Supporting Learners with SEND*, there are many types of assessment activities and tasks. Developing the skills of TAs to undertake specific assessment tasks can increase the resource capacity available to teachers, SENCOs and SEN Practitioners. In reality, TAs working with individual learners or small groups of learners will be making informal assessments all of the time. The information can often be lost as it may not be formally collated or shared. Investing in training and support for TAs so they can complete the assessment function of learning support utilises their insights and maximises impact. You may already be using your TAs to baseline skills or complete tests with learners. They may also be implementing screening assessments linked to interventions. **With appropriate training and ongoing monitoring and quality assurance, such activities can be an effective use of time**. In addition, training TAs to complete targeted class observations can be useful. The resources in this chapter include simple observation verbatim forms which capture a description of what

DOI: 10.4324/9781003179436-6

has been observed during an activity. There are also targeted and timed observation forms, where the TA would be able to indicate, using tally marks, when a particular action was observed during a timed interval. Finally, there is a template for a group observation commentary. The resources can be adapted for use in class, during play or lunchtimes, assembly or any other relevant context.

The key to the assessment function, is that the TA will gather the information as commissioned by the teacher, SENCO or SEN Practitioner and return the information to them for analysis and evaluation. The teacher, SENCO or SEN Practitioner remains responsible for collating and interpreting the information gathered, but it is the TA who will collect the information. Best practice would of course involve a professional dialogue between the TA and the teacher, SENCO or SEN Practitioner to clarify information gathered and to jointly consider professional reflections. The ultimate advantage of this function is that TA time can be used to gather additional information and insights relating to skill acquisition, communication, interaction or learning behaviour.

TA time can also be used to collect the views of learners and their families. Training TAs to interview learners to gather their views about their SEND provision and perceived impact of any resources and interventions, can generate essential information for a teacher, SENCO or SEN Practitioner. Similarly, training and deploying TAs to contact families to complete a structured interview, prepared by the teacher, SENCO or SEN Practitioner can again increase the capacity for this otherwise time-intensive monitoring task. The potential is huge, as long as TAs are trained, supported and prepared for the task.

General Observation Schedule

Observation completed by:

Information requested by:

Date:

Class:

Focus or theme:

What do you anticipate you will see?

Context – describe what is happening at the start of the observation. How many learners and adults are involved?

What are you actually seeing? Capture key points that you notice:

Summary of main points noticed:

Key issues to feed back:

Group Observation Template

Observation completed by:

Information requested by:

Date:

Class:

Focus or theme:

What do you anticipate you will see?

Context – describe what is happening at the start of the observation. How many learners and adults are involved with the group?

What are you actually seeing? Capture key points that you notice:

Positives about the group:

Areas of concern:

Summary of main points noticed:

Key issues to feed back:

Group Observation – Feedback Sheet

Completed by:

Requested by:

Date:

Context:

Group Members	Observed Actions	Points to Feed Back
General Comments:		

Targeted Skills or Behaviour Observation Schedule

Observation completed by:

Information requested by:

Date:

Class:

Focus or theme:

What do you anticipate you will see?

Context – describe what is happening at the start of the observation. How many learners and adults are involved with the group?

What are you actually seeing? Capture key points that you notice:

Strengths:

Areas for development:

Summary of main points noticed:

Key issues to feed back:

Learning Support Observation

Context:

Date:

Completed by:

Information requested by:

Purpose/Theme:

Anticipated Impact:

Actual Impact:

Observation Summary (Notes overleaf)

Positives:

Areas to Develop:

Action Required:

Family Telephone Consultation

Learner Name:

Family Member:

Completed by:

Date:

Purpose:

Question Prompts	Family Response	Actions Required
Does your child like coming to school?		
Do they talk about their learning or any activities?		
What do they think they are good at?		
Are they worried about anything at school?		
How do you think they are getting on at school?		
How would you describe their strengths?		
What do you think they need to work on next?		
Are you worried about anything or have any questions?		

Intervention

The fourth and final of our 4 Functions of Learning Support is that of intervention. As with assessment, the purpose of an intervention is to provide opportunities that may ultimately *remove* a barrier to learning, if that is a possibility. In many ways, the principles of mediation, explored in detail in Chapter 5, are also relevant for TAs delivering an intervention. After all, during the intervention (which could be integrated into the class activity or presented as an additional task in or outside of the classroom), the TA may facilitate a shared mediated learning experience, which should include intentionality, reciprocity, meaning and transcendence. In real terms, the TA will be clear about the purpose and intention of the learning they are trying to create with the individual or small group. They will be dependent on the individual or group responding and engaging with them, and they should always explain in detail what the purpose of the learning task is and how this could be used back in the classroom. Training and deploying TAs to deliver interventions can be an effective use of time.

As with all of the 4 Functions of Learning Support, it is the teacher who should commission the intervention, in partnership with the SENCO or SEN Practitioner and with the learner and their family. It is their combined insight of the learner's strengths and barriers to learning that will determine the nature of the required intervention. Inviting learners to participate in interventions is an essential step to promoting a shared understanding of the purpose of the intervention, for both the teacher and the learner. It can help to encourage the application of learning from one context to another (transcendence) and help to demonstrate the impact of an intervention on learning in the classroom.

The resources in this chapter include sample intervention records which may be useful to help TAs capture attendance and participation during an intervention. However, the key to the effectiveness of this function is not the resources, but the training and support given to TAs as preparation for delivery, combined with the need for ongoing monitoring and quality assurance.

Group Intervention Baseline Record Sheet

Intervention:

Anticipated Impact:

Start Date:

End Date:

Facilitated by:

Learner Name	Starting Point	Actual Impact	Next Steps

Learner Invitation

Dear Khalid,

You are invited to take part in an activity group with 5 other children. The group will meet every week for 5 weeks to take part in a series of games that will last about 30 minutes. The games are chosen to help you remember information. I have noticed that although you listen really well, it is sometimes hard for you to remember lots of things. I hope that by playing these games you will be able to remember more things when you are working in the classroom.

If you have any questions about this please do ask me, but I hope you will enjoy taking part with this group and you will be able to see if it helps you to remember more things!

Keep working hard!

Best wishes

Ms Carter

Implications for SENCOs and SEN Practitioners

TA deployment to assessment and intervention functions can significantly boost the capacity for such tasks in a school or setting. There is huge potential in this application if TAs are regularly trained and supported. Developing these skills with TAs can create opportunities for information- gathering that may otherwise be deferred. Of course, the interpretation and evaluation of the information gathered remains the responsibility of the teacher, SENCO or SEN Practitioner, but the TA, with the right training, can provide essential additional capacity. If you are able to build the skills of your TA workforce to fulfil all of the 4 Functions of Learning Support and, empower your teachers as commissioners of learning support, you will be able to demonstrate the impact of this resource on teaching and learning.

Reflections

- How do you currently plan your TA training programme?
- Are TAs involved in assessment and intervention activities currently?
- Could the 4 Functions of Learning Support provide a useful framework for your teachers and TAs?

References

SEND Assessment: A Strengths-based Framework for Learners with SEND (2021) Judith Carter. Abingdon: Routledge Speechmark.

7. The role of adults

Adults are fundamental to planning SEND provision with purpose, whether this relates to our teachers identifying and implementing appropriate adjustments that enable access to teaching, or through the deployment of TAs to the 4 Functions of Learning Support. But this is not the only contribution that adults make. We know that adults make significant contributions to the learning process of children and young people, albeit intentionally or unintentionally! Whether the nature of their contribution is to provide the stimulus that enables the child to explore and learn by 'active knowledge' and hands-on experience, as Piaget may have argued, or whether they create a shared problem-solving experience or dialectical process, as Vygotsky may have advocated. Either way, adults matter! Therefore, SENCOs and SEN Practitioners, planning provision with purpose, should harness this capacity.

To harness the capacity of your adults, you will first need to audit the resource. This involves gaining knowledge of the individual family contexts of learners as well as reviewing adult capacity at the school or setting. Of course, this includes teachers and TAs but also other adults including administrative staff, lunchtime staff, caretaking and cleaning staff as well as governors, volunteers and external agencies who visit the school and or individual learners. This knowledge is essential, as all adults who interact with the learner have the potential to make a positive or negative contribution to their learning. You will have experienced the impact of a negative 'throwaway' or reactive comment made by an adult and its extensive ripple of impact on a learner. Similarly, the positive impact of an encouraging and genuinely constructive comment. Paul Dix (2017), in his powerful book *When the Adults Change Everything Changes*, reminds us of our collective contribution to change and the need for an authentic restorative approach. He says: "The positive relationship you form with pupils depends on a restorative approach being your default mode" (page 125).

As an advocate of social learning theory, I am mindful of the Vygotskyian construct that development is a process of internalisation, where children observe the application of knowledge, thought, values etc. in the adults around them, and through interaction and a shared learning process they explore and eventually internalise this for themselves. This is highly relevant for SENCOs and SEN Practitioners as it reminds us of the impact that a school culture and family context will have on an individual. If adults within the school or indeed within the family,

DOI: 10.4324/9781003179436-7

present low expectations, disappointment or disillusionment towards any individual learner, then this may be internalised by them themselves. This can trigger a negative self-fulfilling prophecy which impacts on progress and engagement.

To avoid this scenario and to maximise all of our potential resources, we should seek to ensure that the adults surrounding the learner are supported to champion all learners and value their individual learning experiences. For some, this will involve communicating knowledge that promotes understanding of individual difference and neurodiversity. In real terms, this may involve whole staff training on autism, attachment and trauma, cerebral palsy or sensory processing etc., to ensure that all adults have an insight into individual ways of being or particular barriers to learning that may be experienced by some in the school. Similarly, establishing whole staff training that promotes inclusive values, high aspirations and the importance of difference could be useful, as this will help to determine a shared language of expectations, which in turn promotes a collective code of conduct and interaction where no learner or family are made to feel excluded or less important. Such steps will help to mitigate any 'unintentional' negative impact that adults could have on learners, but how can you maximise the intentional positive impact of adults on learners?

Parents and carers

The Education Endowment Foundation report and guidance into *Working with Parents to Support Children's Learning*, published in 2018, identifies four key recommendations for schools to apply in order to promote effective parental engagement. First, to critically review *how* they work with parents. Second, to provide practical strategies that can be used to support learning at home. Third, to tailor communications to encourage positive dialogue about learning and finally, offer more sustained and intensive support where needed. The research noted that although there is significant research to support the important contribution that families play with regards to children's learning, there was less research into 'how' greater family engagement could be achieved.

In 2020, as a result of the global coronavirus pandemic, schools in the United Kingdom were required to move to remote learning for the majority of their learners. Literally overnight, the majority of learners were expected to be taught at home by both family members and school staff. Despite the unprecedented challenge, this national necessity to stay at home appeared to advance family engagement with learning dramatically. Ironically, the recommendations of the Education Endowment Foundation's *Working with Parents* report, which pre-pandemic perhaps seemed less achievable, became an essential requirement! **For many, the COVID lockdowns triggered greater connections with families and an almost 'collegiate' alliance between staff and families, combined with an empathetic respect and shared humanity, that perhaps had not been seen before on this scale.** The durability of this connection is not clear, but the insight that it provided was vast. SENCOs and SEN Practitioners seeking to plan provision with purpose, may seek to utilise the lessons from this experience and attempt to maximise and sustain effective communication, resources and collaborative approaches with learners and their families. Nurturing capacity for support and consistent approaches for learning in school and at home will increase the effectiveness of SEND provision. **Empowering parents and carers to provide adjustments, support and interventions that mirror those available in school, as part of their family experience, will maximise opportunities for learners.** After all, however long a school day may feel, the majority of a learner's time is spent with or under the supervision of their family.

The resources that follow are offered as a starting point to aid communication with families regarding the 7 Cs Learning Portfolio. In addition, there is a trifold leaflet that provides some examples of adjustments, support and intervention ideas that could be used at home. Obviously, these can be personalised and adapted for your school or setting or indeed for individual families.

The 7 Cs Learning Portfolio

By Judith Carter

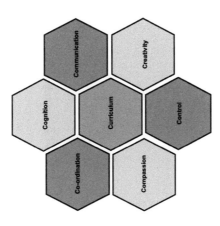

The 7 Cs Learning Portfolio helps to define barriers to learning and inform action. It provides a language of assessment that helps us all to consider 'why' a learner is having difficulties with the curriculum. It is not always enough to provide 'more' maths if a learner is finding maths difficult. We may need to support their language, memory or processing. The 7 Cs Learning Portfolio gives us a language to do this.

What next?

You might like to...

- Encourage your child to talk about their strengths and difficulties

- Ask them what they think they are good at

- Tell them when you notice what they are good at

Families know their children the best and we want to work with you and your child to support their learning.

We will be using this language of assessment to encourage your child to identify strengths and areas for development. We hope we can do this together.

If you have any questions about this approach please speak to your child's teacher or SENCO.

A strengths-based approach

Information for Families

Curriculum

- English
- Maths
- Science
- Art & Music
- History & Geography
- Computing
- PE & Sport

If you would like to find out more about the 7 Cs, we have a User Guide which describes what each of the skills may look like. This might help you and your child to talk about their strengths and difficulties.

The idea of the 7 Cs Learning Portfolio has been taken from a book called *SEND Assessment: A Strengths-based Framework for Learners with SEND* by Judith Carter, published by Routledge Speechmark 2021.

7 Cs Learning Portfolio

In our school we are using the 7 Cs Learning Portfolio to help identify pupil strengths and barriers to learning. The 7 Cs Learning Portfolio provides a *language* of assessment that we can all use.

- The 7 Cs Learning Portfolio includes the curriculum as one of the 'Cs' but also defines 6 extra 'Cs' that are essential for learning.

- Within each 'C' there are 7 skills.

- We can talk about each skill and together agree strengths and areas for development.

- This will help us plan next steps.

Together with your child, we will all identify 3 strengths and 3 areas for development.

We also have a Progress Tracker that we can use to identify 'starting points' and capture improvements.

Cognition
- Working Memory
- Speed of Processing
- Inference
- Anticipation
- Reflection
- Evaluation
- Analysis

Communication
- Expressive Vocabulary
- Articulation
- Language & Understanding
- Collaboration Conversation
- Listening
- Social Communication
- Social Interaction

Creativity
- Generate ideas
- Problem solving
- Attention
- Motivation
- Making things
- Courage
- Trust

Control
- Self Regulation
- Behaviour for Learning
- Anxiety Management
- Confidence
- Resilience
- Language of Emotions
- Independence

Compassion
- Friendships
- Turn Taking
- Empathy
- Sense of Justice
- Self Esteem & Wellbeing
- Self Efficacy
- Support for Others

Co-ordination
- Fine Motor Skills
- Gross Motor Skills
- Sensory
- Mobility
- Stability & Balance
- Posture
- Sensory Processing

Supporting Learning Using the 7 Cs Learning Portfolio

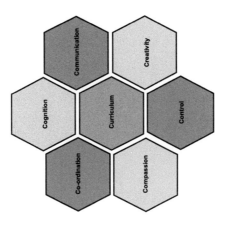

A strengths-based approach

Information for Families

Curriculum

- Whenever time allows, read with your child whatever their age. Take it in turns to read, talk about the story and what might happen next.

- Help to structure writing using sentence starters and create a word list that they can use.

- When learning spellings, give them 3 versions of the same word and ask them to highlight the one that is spelt correctly.

- Use visual prompts to help with maths. Blue tac can be used for counters.

- Point out money, fractions and time in real life situations.

- Promote a love of nature and the world around them. Encourage thinking and discussion about all they see and hear.

What next?

Families do, of course, know their children the best and we want to work with you and your child to support their learning.

When time allows, give these suggestions a try and come and talk to us about how you are getting on and what you have noticed.

Encourage your child to identify 3 strengths and 3 areas for development and continue to celebrate their achievements.

The 7 Cs Learning Portfolio was written by Judith Carter and published by Routledge Speechmark 2021

Compassion

- Talk to them about friends and rehearse icebreakers for new situations.

- Use stories or films to explore different points of view.

- Encourage them to identify what they think they have done well at that day. If necessary tell them 2 things you noticed, but ask them to choose what they think.

- Use structured choices so they learn to make decisions and know that their thoughts matter.

Co-ordination

- Develop fine motor skills by drawing, cutting, threading, sorting objects and rehearse vertical, horizontal and circular movements in isolation to help with letter formation.

- Rehearse throwing, kicking, catching a ball and standing, hopping, jumping, running as well as keeping balance.

- Look out for any sensitivities to loud sounds, lights, tastes, smells or items to touch. Also look to see if your child seeks these experiences. Talk to their Teacher if you do see these.

- Get regular sight and hearing tests.

7 Cs Learning Portfolio

In our school we are using the 7 Cs Learning Portfolio to help identify pupil strengths and barriers to learning. The 7 Cs Learning Portfolio provides a *language* of assessment that we can all use.

Supporting learning can involve making *adjustments* or tweaks to the way information is shared. It can also involve specific *resources, equipment or support*. And at times it may involve targeted action or *intervention*. In school we try to offer a combination of adjustments, support and intervention to overcome or remove barriers to learning.

We know that families also want to support learning for their children, so this leaflet gives some examples of actions that may be able to integrate in to family life or homework. The suggestions are offered for consideration, but please feel free to modify these or talk to your child's Teacher or SENCO if you would like further information.

Above all, continue to listen, love and encourage your children promoting their individual strengths, skills and confidence.

Cognition

- Use short and concise information and ask your child to repeat back key points.
- Ensure they have sufficient time to complete tasks
- Ask questions rather than give answers.
- Scaffold and support their understanding by giving the next step but resist solving it for them!
- Play games such as snap, pairs, missing objects, jigsaws, spot the difference etc.

Communication

- Say their name before giving instructions.
- Check out their understanding of words when reading or talking.
- Share stories by reading or listening to audio books or watching films, Discuss the words.
- Teach conversation modelling my turn, your turn
- Play listening games where information and thoughts are shared.

Creativity

- Create, make, bake and build with a range of materials!
- Encourage your child to share thoughts and ideas
- Share 'what if?' questions so all family members consider responses and possibilities.
- Celebrate random and out of the box thinking!
- Praise effort and achievement defining what it is that you like
- Promote a 'keep trying' approach even if mistakes our made.

Control

- Stay calm when your child is angry or distressed and try to gently label their feelings and remind them of actions they could take.
- If your child is anxious listen to their concerns. Ask what they could do to help themselves? Ask if there is anything they would like you to do, but try not to offer the solution for them!
- Promote their own capacity to cope and control—tell them that you believe in them.
- When they are calm, talk about feelings and actions to take when feelings overwhelm us.

Teachers and TAs

Much of our time within this book has already focused on the provision capacity of teachers and TAs. The core implication for SENCOs and SEN Practitioners is to promote the potential of teachers as commissioners of SEND provision. If teachers perceive themselves as commissioners of SEND provision, be that of their own adjustments or tweaks that enable curriculum access for all, or the offer of resources and support from TAs working within the 4 Functions of Learning Support, to commissioning interventions that they feel will target learning outcomes for individual learners, then they have 'ownership' of SEND provision. SEND provision should not be something that happens because of the SENCO or SEN Practitioner, it should happen because teachers, as the professionals responsible for the teaching and learning of all in their class, have commissioned it. This simple shift can empower both the teacher role, the TA and the SENCO and SEN Practitioner role, not to mention enhance the learning experience of the child or young person.

Ensuring that teachers have sufficient knowledge and experience of the diverse range of learner needs, in order to commission SEND provision, is essential. This should form the bedrock of your approach to continued professional development (CPD.) As part of your role as SENCO or SEN Practitioner, it will be necessary to evaluate professional knowledge and confidence regarding SEND and to plan CPD opportunities that develop capacity and skills. The resources contained in this section include a CPD planner that may be useful to you as you audit and plan for development tasks. The purpose of this planner is to capture the rationale as well as the range of tasks selected each term. The use of these tools is of course optional, but do ensure that SEND CPD planning is explicit in terms of its intent, implementation and of course, impact.

SEND CPD Activity Planner – Willow Tree Primary Academy Annual Planner

Academic Year: 2020–21: Autumn 2020

What are we doing?	Why this and not something else? (SIDP and/or Provision Mapping)	How will it be delivered? (Modality)	Who will take part?	When will this take place?	Who will facilitate?	How much will it cost?	Impact and follow-up?
Understanding Autism – whole school training day	SIDP priority emerged from increased numbers of new pupils with autism.	Trainer-led & workshops	All staff – teachers, co-educators, midday assistants, clerical and caretaking	25-10-20 Inset Day.	Keynote Speaker: Claire Jordan	£600	
TA Training on Coaching for Kids	SIDP priority: improving the quality of support and questioning used by learning mentors.	Workshops	All co-educators, SENCO, SEN Governor	Termly training within monthly team meeting session, 4-1-21 and 5-5-21.	SENCO, using the resources from *Life Coaching for Kids* by Nikki Giant	No additional costs beyond purchase price of book (£19).	
Can the use of metacognitive questioning improve independent learning?	SIDP priority: improving learning and independence.	Trainer-led & workshop	Teaching staff	Twilight 22-11-20 Plus 3 themed staff meetings as follow-up, 29-11-20, 5-2-20, 8-5-20.	EP to lead Twilight Deputy Head & SENCO facilitate staff meetings	£350 EP cost	
Life Coaching for Kids by Nikki Giant is the Autumn term book for teacher book club	Recommended by EP for practical resources and accessible theory on coaching approaches.	Self-directed	Book club identifies a book that every teacher will read within a term.	6 copies available from 3-9-20. Expectation that will be read and passed on by half term.	SENCO will launch at staff meeting on 3-9-20 and allocate initial 6 copies, and launch the exchange on 25-10-20.	6 copies of book purchased (£19 x 6 = £114)	

SEND CPD Activity – School Planner
Academic Year:

What are we doing?	Why this and not something else? (SIDP and/or Provision Mapping)	Who will take part?	When will this take place?	Who will facilitate?	How much will it cost?

This chapter also includes a collection of resources that may provide a useful starting point for staff. You will see a collection of 'Professional Prompt' sheets that provide an overview to some barriers to learning. There is also a template to encourage you to develop your own summary sheets for staff. There are also some 'information boxes' which are intended to be printed, cut out and folded into boxes for placement on desks or tables. Each box provides practical suggestions relating to the Code of Practice four categories of need that teachers could apply to meet the needs of learners. I acknowledge that these may only appeal to those of you who, like me, still like 'paper' and are drawn to 'gimmicks as a way 'in' for staff. If this is not you, please ignore the presentation of the information, but the information itself may still serve a purpose, so as always, feel free to modify and amend!

Professional Prompt Sheet: Working Memory

What is it?

Working memory is part of short-term memory and refers to **our capacity to 'hold' and manipulate information.** It is the part of our memory before it goes into storage. Auditory working memory is often measured using forward and backward digit span tasks, where pupils are asked to repeat number sequences. Auditory working memory is used to recall spoken information or instructions. Visual working memory can be measured by showing a picture or series of images and asking pupils to identify the picture or image from several options. Visual working memory is used when copying information from the board.

Working memory capacity can vary between people and there is no link with intelligence. So you can be a high attainer and have a small working memory. Research suggests that capacity can be improved slightly up until the age of 14, but the focus is primarily on efficiency, support and alternative methods of holding information such as note-taking, mind mapping and technological aids.

What might I see in the classroom?

- The pupil will be listening but when asked to begin work does not know what tasks have been set.
- A pupil may laboriously copy from the board but could repeat words or letters whilst doing so.
- The pupil may not enjoy reading as they can read words but struggle to recall what they are reading so have no pleasure from reading.
- When asked to collect several items they are unable to do so.
- They may struggle to sustain friendships and keep up with 'banter.

What action can I take to overcome or remove the barrier?

- Ensure that task instructions are simple and concise.
- Ask pupils to paraphrase key instructions.
- Encourage pupils to take a photo of the information on the board so it is in front of them.
- Teach note-taking and or the use of mind mapping.
- Reduce memory overload providing prompts and recapping.

Professional Prompt Sheet: Speed of Processing

What is it?

Speed of processing refers to **how quickly a pupil can assimilate or take on information.** This directly impacts on an individual rate or speed of working. For some pupils, they can assimilate new information quickly, but others need additional time.

What might I see in the classroom?

- A slower speed of processing implies that a pupil may need additional time to formulate or answer questions.
- They may find it difficult to 'follow' or keep up with information.
- They may become overwhelmed and anxious or appear to switch off, as they have 'lost' pace with the lesson.
- If they process information quickly, they may become distracted, as they are ready for the next challenge.

What action can I take to overcome the barrier?

- Give additional time for formulating and answering questions by providing advanced warning or returning to the pupil for an answer.
- Provide visual prompts and encourage paraphrasing of information.
- Provide activities intended to increase reaction time, e.g., playing snap, Hungry Hippos or any time-related task.
- Consider if the pupil is eligible for additional time in exams.
- Reassure the pupil that there is nothing 'wrong' with them, they simply need time to take on information.

Professional Prompt Sheet: Executive Functioning

What is it?

Executive function skills are **higher order cognitive or thinking skills**. They include skills such as planning, anticipation, inference, deduction, reflection, time management and evaluation. They encourage 'hypothesis' formation and 'wonder.'

What might I see in the classroom?

- A child with limited executive functioning skills may be fairly impulsive and reactive, tending to 'do' without thinking.
- They may not make 'connections' between tasks or previous learning.
- A child may repeat seemingly 'dangerous' actions without any consideration of risk.
- Work ideas may be sporadic, disordered and chaotic.
- Tasks may be completed in no time or not completed in the time.
- A child may not be able to provide a rationale for their thinking or describe the strategy applied.

What action can I take to overcome the barrier?

- Make explicit the implicit! Describe the connections and provide a rationale for tasks.
- Sign-post learning and refer to prior learning.
- Provide writing frames, planning grids and layout templates to aid organisation.
- Use questioning to promote thinking and 'connect' responses.
- Give advanced warning to time remaining.

Professional Prompt Sheet: Phonics and Phonological Awareness

What is it?

Phonics is an understanding of the correlation between sounds and the letter symbol. It requires visual recall and 'matching' of sounds to letters. Applying phonic skills to aid reading involves sounding out and blending sounds together, looking at letters in words.

Phonological awareness is an auditory skill and should be taught without visual prompts. **It is the skill of 'hearing' sounds in words**. Phonological skills involve synthesis – building sounds to create a word, e.g., c–a–t = cat. And segmentation – deconstructing sounds from a word, e.g., cat = c–a–t.

It is the combination of phonics (visual) and phonological skills (auditory) that enable reading and spelling that does not specifically rely on recall or sight vocabulary.

What might I see in the classroom?

- Spelling errors provide the greatest insight into phonics and phonological awareness. If the child is developing skills their spelling mistakes will be phonetically regular and 'logical.' Where it appears that 'random' letters have been selected, a child may be recalling symbols incorrectly or simply not hearing the sounds.
- Great verbal ideas but minimal writing. A child may simply not know 'how' to write the sounds or may not be able to recall what the sound looks like. Alternatively, they may not be able to 'hear' the sounds and match these to letters.
- Laborious reading, without fluency or accuracy.
- Anxiety or avoidance with reading or writing tasks.
- Disruptive behaviour and task refusal.

What action can I take to overcome the barrier?

- Explicitly teach phonics by visually rehearsing sound identification from written letters. Similarly teach phonological awareness auditorily by asking the child or young person to identify sounds they can hear in spoken phonically regular words (no pictures.)
- Provide a visual prompt to aid recall of letter symbols. This can be presented alphabetically or possibly more usefully within a qwerty keyboard layout.
- Target 'quick wins' by focusing on a smaller number of sounds such as b, m, c, s, n, t, p, I, a, e, o, u, which can combine to form 2 and 3 letter C-V-C words.
- Rehearse phonic recognition and synthesis and segmentation skills (phonological awareness) for a few minutes every day, starting with sounds that are known and adding additional sounds.

Professional Prompt Sheet: Fine and Gross Motor Skills

What is it?

Fine motor skills are controlled movements using distal muscles in the hand and fingers. Such as writing, colouring, cutting, drawing, pinching, threading and weaving.

Gross motor skills are larger controlled movements, using larger muscles in the body, arms and legs. Including standing, walking, running, hopping, jumping, skipping and throwing, catching, kicking and rolling a ball. Core control is also essential for seating, balancing and twisting.

Fluency and accuracy with fine and gross motor skills is the aim.

What might I see in the classroom?

- Difficulties with letter formation and fluency of pencil movements.
- Lack of accuracy when cutting or colouring.
- 'Messy' work when sticking or crafting.
- Slouching, fidgeting and laying over the table rather than sitting upright.
- 'Clumsy' uncoordinated movements.

What action can I take to overcome the barrier?

- Explicit teaching of the skill and opportunities for rehearsal.
- Revise pencil grip and letter formation.
- Rehearse vertical, horizontal and circular movements of different sizes in isolation.
- Posture cushion and or feet guide (to remind where feet should be.)
- Craft activities and rehearsal of movements, e.g.: Brain Gym

Professional Prompt Sheet: Impulsivity and Attention

What is it?

Impulsivity is an immediate urge to react. It is an action, thought or comment that is 'blurted out' or made without forethought.

Attention is selective concentration or sustained focus combined with the ability to screen out or filter other thoughts, actions or environmental stimuli to pursue or attend to a specific task.

What might I see in the classroom?

- A child or young person may 'constantly' blurt out a response or thought during whole class discussions.
- They may 'flit' between tasks, sustaining attention for a short amount of time.
- A child or young person may never actually 'finish' a task, as they are constantly moving between activities.
- They may be distractible and 'notice' all that is around them, responding to sounds, sights or comments.
- They may verbalise their thoughts and seemingly engage in 'constant chatter.'

What action can I take to overcome the barrier?

- Explicitly teach task completion even if this means tasks are completed within a few minutes.
- Play games or activities that require 'pausing' or waiting. Traditional games such as musical statues and 'what's the time Mr Wolf' involve 'holding' a position at a specific time. For older students use Drama and the concept of 'freezing' and maintaining a position.
- Baseline the attention span for the child or young person and plan to change activities prior to the end of their span. Encourage physical movement between tasks.
- Create a box of short activities or flip over books, where activities can be completed for a few minutes and then flipped over and changed. Integrate tasks such as jigsaw puzzles, spot the difference, pairs and colour by number tasks into the curriculum.

Professional Prompt Sheet: Social Communication and Social Interaction

What is it?

Social communication skills are the skills used by an individual to communicate. Including, use of speech, intonation, eye contact, awareness of personal space, turn-taking etc. These are 'output' skills.

Social interaction skills are the skills used by an individual to respond or react to communication. Including, language comprehension, gestures, listening, eye contact, inference, etc. These are 'input' skills.

What might I see in the classroom?

- A child or young person may not know 'how' to 'join' in a conversation or activity. They may use an inappropriate action such as pinching, punching or screaming to initiate interaction.
- Literal interpretation and confusion over 'banter' or popular social terminology.
- Invasion or inappropriate use of personal space or working area.
- Hoarding of group or shared equipment.
- Social isolation or bullying.

What action can I take to overcome the barrier?

- Make explicit the implicit. Do not assume understanding and ensure that the rationale for actions or routines is shared.
- Clarify phrases or sayings signposting where there is or is not a literal interpretation.
- Identify a small circle of friends to support a child who appears to be isolated.
- Explicitly teach an 'opening' sentence such as 'can I play?' or teach and rehearse 'icebreakers' with older children and young people.
- Rehearse social expectations using social stories or social scenario discussions.

Professional Prompt Sheet: Anxiety

What is it?

Anxiety is a feeling of unease and worry often associated with uncertainty. It can be a useful and protective feeling as it triggers a response in the body to warn of risk or potential danger. However, for many children, young people and adults, anxiety can be experienced repeatedly and associated with 'non-threatening' triggers. Instead, anxious thoughts are generated which in turn generate anxious feelings. These feelings promote the desire to avoid the source of the anxious thought. Avoidance increases and reinforces further anxious thoughts and negative associations. This is known as the anxiety cycle.

Anxiety can generate automatic negative thoughts which dominate and debilitate thinking.

What might I see in the classroom?

- Anxiety can present in various forms. Utter fear or terror evidenced by screaming or crying. Refusal to engage with requests. Withdrawal and retreat such as hiding under a table or leaving a room. At other times anxiety can present as anger and aggression, typifying the 'fight or flight' type response.
- Children and young people may experience physical symptoms and complain of feeling unwell.
- Depending on the trigger for the anxious thought, a child or young person may not attend school or will 'forget' their kit or equipment.
- Some children may seek to manage their anxiety by talking or singing to themselves, rocking, running, biting nails, going to the toilet, washing hands or attempting to distract others and therefore themselves.
- Declining levels of participation and attainment as they are simply pre-occupied with the source of their anxious thoughts.

What action can I take to overcome the barrier?

- 'Notice' that the source of the concern is anxiety, not 'naughtiness'.
- Remind the child or young person that they are safe. Attempt to label the presenting behaviour by saying, "I wonder if you are feeling anxious now?" Ask them what might help them to manage these feelings? Encourage them to pursue an action previously identified for such times.
- Talk about anxiety as a cycle, 'modelling' and acknowledging anxious thoughts and the connected feelings. Link these thoughts to a positive action that could be taken.
- Attempt to establish a language of feelings, including anxiety. Find out about Cognitive Behavioural Techniques including thinking bias and overcoming automatic negative thoughts.

Professional Prompt Sheet: Attachment

What is it?

Attachment theory originates from developmental psychology and **it explores the relationship between a child and their care giver and considers the impact that this has on interaction and risk taking**. If a child forms a secure attachment, they are more likely to explore, connect with others and branch out independently from that secure base. Less secure attachments can lead to difficulties with trust, sharing, sense of self-worth and difficulties forming and ending relationships.

Attachment disorder is a medical diagnosis which describes patterns of behaviour considered to result from a lack of developmental bonds with a primary caregiver during early childhood.

What might I see in the classroom?

- The child or young person may excessively seek attention from adults and or children and then 'push' them away or reject them.
- They may struggle to form and sustain friendships. On formation a friendship could become intense as the child may become controlling and resent connections with others. This could end abruptly in rejection.
- The child may have difficulties 'trusting' others and may have low self-esteem.
- They may operate with heightened vigilance resulting in shorter attention and distractibility.
- A child or young person may appear to have heightened emotions or show no emotional response.
- They may struggle to sustain friendships and keep up with 'banter.

What action can I take to overcome the barrier?

- Offer a consistent and reliable response.
- Ensure that praise is meaningful and related to action.
- Promote fairness and equity in all interactions.
- Separate the child or young person from the behaviour, making explicit that any negativity about their behaviour is not about them as a whole.
- Try to 'notice' the small things, emphasising that they 'matter' and show interest towards their thoughts and actions.
- Monitor friendships and attempt to broker positive opportunities for collaboration with peers.
- Start each day afresh.

Professional Prompt Sheet: Sensory Processing

What is it?

Sensory processing refers to the way the central nervous system organises and responds to sensory information gained from the environment. For some they can have a hyper or magnified response, whereby sensory experiences are perceived too intensely. For others, they may have a hypo or under experience, resulting in repetitive seeking of the sensory information. For example, humming and singing at all times could link to a 'need' to seek auditory information.

There are 8 sensory processes: Visual, Auditory, Tactile, Olfactory, Oral, Vestibular, Proprioception and Interoception.

Sensory processing experiences differ for and within each individual. A child or young person may have a hypo response to one sensory experience and a hyper to another whilst integrating other experiences. Responses need to be monitored over time and across contexts.

What might I see in the classroom?

- A hyper (over) auditory processing experience could result in a child covering their ears or seeking to withdraw from the stimuli. A hypo (under) auditory processing experience could result in the child tapping, singing, humming or constantly talking to generate sound.
- Sucking or chewing fingers, thumb, hair, pencil tops or sleeves could suggest a hypo (under) oral sensory experience.
- Repetitively staring at lights or switching them on and off, could suggest a hypo response to visual sensory information.
- Leaning across others when sitting on the carpet area or falling in to others could suggest limited (hypo) proprioception (sense of self in relation to space) or hypo vestibular (balance.)

What action can I take to overcome the barrier?

- Mindfully 'notice' the sensory demands of the learning environment and filter out unnecessary information.
- Encourage the use of headphones, ear defenders or sunglasses to filter out sounds and light.
- Provide opportunities to process sensory information through activities that generate experience.
- Liaise with parents/carers to check out if observed behaviours occur in other contexts.

Professional Prompt Sheet:

What is it?

What might I see in the classroom?

What action can I take to overcome the barrier?

SEN Support Building Block: Cognition & Learning

Executive Functioning

- Use writing frames and planners
- Play games which involve 'pausing'
- Stop and ask anticipatory questions
- Teach risk assessment

Maths

- Prompts to aid number sequencing
- Reminder cards with key facts and language
- Pre-learning of conceptual language
- Visual prompts to aid recall

Speed of Processing

- Give sufficient time
- Play reaction time games to develop speed
- Avoid setting the child up to 'fail'
- Ask a question and come back for answer

Working Memory

- Paraphrase work instructions
- Use concise information with a visual prompt
- Place information to be copied in front of pupil
- Teach note-taking
- Verbally record instructions for independent play-back

Reading, Writing, Spelling

- Rehearsal of letter sounds to fluency
- Synthesis and segmentation of sounds heard in words
- Visual Qwerty or alphabet letter card prompt
- Rehearse formation of vertical, horizontal & circular movements

Independent Thinking

- Ask questions
- Make connections explicit
- Encourage choice
- Ask pupil to give a rationale: tell me why?

SEN Support Building Block: Communication & Interaction

Speech (Expressive Vocabulary)

- Alternative means of communication – pictures, signs, gestures, key words
- 'Can I play?' card or gesture for peer interaction
- Stay calm and give time for expression

Social Interaction (input)

- Social stories to rehearse social expectations
- Teach 'exceptions' and points of view
- Make explicit the implicit: teach key phrases
- Talk about worries or confusion

Social Communication (output)

- Teach key phrases or ice breakers
- Make explicit the implicit including: personal space, turn taking
- Notice eye contact but do not force it
- Peer supporter, buddy or circle of friends

Listening & Attention

- Concise information
- Vary voice intonation
- Use name of child at start of instruction
- Short & varied tasks – have a box of 3 minute tasks

Language (Receptive Vocabulary)

- Ensure accessible & concise language
- Check out understanding by asking child to paraphrase
- Combine words with a visual prompt or gesture

Friendships

- Circle of Friends or Peer Pyramid of friends
- Explicit teaching of key phrases and ice-breakers
- Explicit teaching of giving & receiving compliments
- Facilitate shared working broker 'connections'

SEN Support Building Block: Social, Emotional & Mental Health

Behaviour
- Identify the 'motives' for the behaviour
- Attention? Power? Revenge? Avoidance?
- Fear of failure or exploration?
- Praise the positive

Social Development
- Time for unstructured interaction & play
- Social stories & enrichment opportunities
- Conversation, vocabulary, exploration
- Positive role models

Anxiety
- Anxious thoughts, lead to avoidance, leads to anxious thoughts
- 'Notice' and name anxious thoughts
- Explore 'likelihood' of anxious thought happening
- Promote self help techniques: mindfulness, counting, finger tracing

Mental Health
- Talk about mental & physical health
- Teach concepts of resiliency and self
- Ask child to identify strengths
- Identification & management of fears

Emotional Development
- 'Notice' feelings: "I wonder if you feel?"
- Picture or photo presentation of feelings
- Link an action with a feeling
- Value all emotions

Attachment
- Remain consistent, fair and predictable to promote trust
- Every day is a fresh start
- Listen, talk, listen
- Broker friendships via shared projects

SEN Support Building Block: Physical & Sensory

Mobility
- Create space for aids
- Notice any height difference and risk from physical exclusion from group discussion, peer also sits on chair
- Promote independence and utilise peer support at play where possible
- Value individual difference

Gross Motor
- Audit skills of walking, running, jumping, hopping, throwing, catching, kicking and rolling a ball
- Rehearse skills developing fluency and accuracy
- Isolate skills for rehearsal e.g., pedalling before riding a bike

Fine Motor
- Rehearse vertical, horizontal and circular movements in isolation prior to letter formation
- Develop fluency and accuracy with drawing, cutting, painting, threading, weaving type tasks
- At times use alternative means of recording: voice recorder, film, peer or adult scribe, typing

Sensory Processing
- Notice 'hyper' (over) or 'hypo' (under) responses to sensory information
- Filter 'hyper' stimuli by using headphones, sunglasses, work station
- Rehearse and explore hypo sensory information
- Vary posture – lay on floor, peanut ball, bean bag

Sensory Impairment - VI, HI MSI
- Read Professional reports & ask Questions
- Utilise 'other' senses
- Ask child and family for preferences & adjustments
- Maximise use of technology

Co-ordination & Balance
- Develop fluency and accuracy of movements via regular rehearsal
- Follow a structured programme such as Sensory Circuits
- Play games that promote balance: musical statues
- Place a wobble board under the desk to rehearse co-ordinated feedback

SEN Support Building Block: Code of Practice

Identification of SEN

- Children can fall behind in their learning for all sorts of reasons...SEN is only one reason. Others include, EAL, low attainment, absence, LAC, bereavement, medical needs
- A child has SEN if they have "a learning difficulty or disability that calls for special educational provision"
- Special educational provision is defined as "additional to or different from the differentiated curriculum"

Assess, Plan, Do & Review

- SEN Support should be informed using the assess, plan, do & review cycle, known as the graduated approach
- Class & subject teachers, working with the SENCO, should collaborate with parents/carers and the child to assess, plan, do and review SEN Support
- This can be captured in any format

SEN Information Report & Local Offer

- The Local Offer is a one-stop shop detailing provision & services for children & families
- The Local Authority in each local area co-ordinates this on behalf of the whole area.
- Schools & settings contribute by writing an SEN information report detailing how SEN is identified and the provision that is offered.
- The SEN information report is on the school website & linked to the Local Offer

SEN Support & EHCP

- From 0-25 years old a child or young person can be identified as having SEN
- When identified SEN Support is triggered and a category of need identified
- A small percentage of children and young people may have an Education, Health and Care plan, following an EHC needs assessment

Categories of Need

- Single category of need, with 4 areas of need: Cognition & Learning, Communication & Interaction, Social, Emotional & Mental Health, Physical and Sensory
- The category of need is informed by the provision that is offered, not a description of the child

Quality First Teaching

- The class or subject Teacher are responsible for the teaching and learning of pupils with SEN even when the pupil is working with a TA
- Access to a differentiated curriculum is the entitlement of all learners. It is not SEN Support
- SEN Support is built on a foundation of quality first teaching, but is additional to or different from the differentiated curriculum

SEN Support Building Block: Equality Act 2010

7 Protected Characteristics

- The Equality Act 2010 brings together related equality legislation
- The 7 protected characteristics of the Equality Act are: sex, race, disability, religion or belief, sexual orientation, gender reassignment, pregnancy or maternity
- There are 2 duties: the **public sector duty** which is a general duty and **specific** duties

Disabled Definition

- A person has a disability if they have "a physical or mental impairment which has a substantial and long-term adverse effect on their ability to carry out normal day-to-day activities"
- Long-term = Over 1 year and 1 day
- Substantial = More than minor or trivial

Prohibited Conduct

- The Equality Act 2010 states that it is unlawful to **Directly Discriminate, Indirectly Discriminate, Victimise or Harass** a person linked to a protected characteristic
- Disabled pupils must not be discriminated against *linked to a disability*; and schools must not fail to make *reasonable adjustments* (which are anticipatory)
- A parent/Carer can make a claim of disability discrimination to the First-tier Tribunal (SEN and Disability)

Specific Duty

This requires schools and settings to:

- Publish information to demonstrate how they comply with the public sector duty
- To prepare and publish equality objectives (this can be in any format including within the SDP)

Public Sector Duty

Those subject to this general duty must have **due regard** to the need to:

- Eliminate unlawful discrimination, harassment and victimisation
- Advance equality of opportunity between different groups
- Foster good relations between different groups

Accessibility Plan

This plan (reviewed every 3 years) sets out how, over time, the school will:

- increase **access to the curriculum** for disabled pupils;
- improve the **physical environment** to increase access for disabled pupils
- ensure access to **written information**

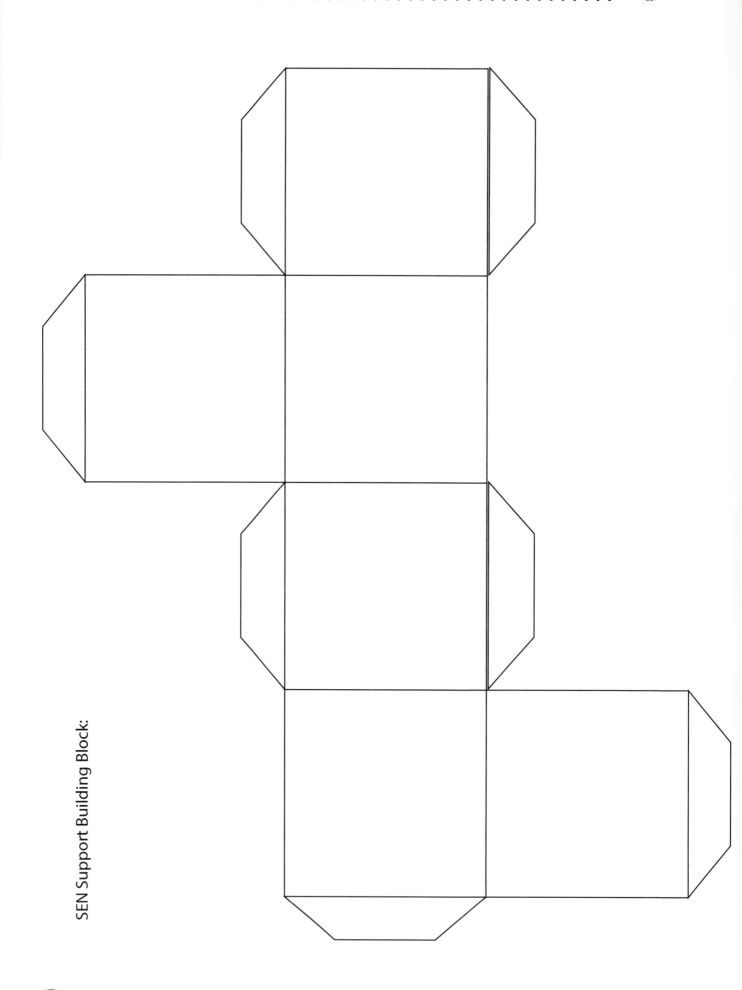

SEN Support Building Block:

Supporting subject teachers in secondary settings to 'hold' information about all of their learners with SEND can be a significant challenge. A maths teacher may teach five different classes a day, each containing a number of learners with SEND and a further five different classes the following day. To aid the communication of need and indeed to promote relevant adjustments or support for each learner, a practical strategy sheet and class list has been included. This was originally developed for subject teachers in secondary schools as part of my research project completed years ago, but can be adapted to any context including to help supply teachers, to gain an overview of primary or class needs. The class list can be completed to show the range of needs within the class, and by turning the sheet over, the teacher has access to some suggestions for adjustments and support that could help to 'overcome' the identified barrier to learning. All of these resources can be adapted and modified to suit your own systems of recording and communication in school. For example, consider merging the practical strategy sheet into your electronic class list or register if that works more effectively for you.

Practical Support Strategies to Overcome Barriers to Learning

Support Strategies	1. Literacy	2. Learning	3. Listening/ Attention	4. Speech/ Language	5. Behaviour/ Control	6. Confidence/ Emotion	7. Social Skills/ Communication	8. Organisation	9. Physical	10. Sensory
A	Use of mind map to record key ideas	Concise 2- or 3-part instructions	Ask student to paraphrase instructions	Provision of vocabulary list with opportunities to rehearse	Positive engagement using student name	Immediate feedback on work tasks and approach to learning	Make explicit the implicit! Be aware of literal examples	Use of visual timetable (symbols or colour coded)	Consider seating position, in relation to classroom	Provision of materials in alternative font size and colouring
B	Access to peer or adult scribe or reader	Explicit revision of prior learning	Positive praise and engagement via use of name	Summarise tasks using visual prompt cards	Positive rewards system linked to whole school policy	Facilitate peer support via seating plan	Structure group or paired activities	Provide homework instructions at the start of the lesson	Access to support equipment, e.g. sloping boards (use of A3 lever arch file)	Seating adjustment according to sensory barrier, e.g. deaf in one ear
C	IT tools to support recording, e.g. laptop, audio recorder	Practical apparatus (blue tack counters)	Give student a 'role' – active engagement in task	Give visual demonstration of task	Direct engagement via role allocation (positive re-direction)	Ask student to identify what they did well at after each lesson	Use of visual prompts and real-life examples	Pictorial and written labels of equipment	Consideration of posture	Ask student to paraphrase work instructions
D	Provide photocopy of homework or task instructions	Visual cues and aids (pictorial task cards)	'Turn to your partner' instructions within class input	Access to peer models/ supporters	Reminder of class rules/ code of conduct to all students	Ensure task appropriate to needs, using must, should, could analysis	Provide advanced notice of change of task or lesson end	Verbal or visual equipment check list	Ensure access to equipment – use of peer partner or LSA to support	Targeted peer support – reader or scribe
E	Provision of key word cards, linked to subject area or topic	Alternative means of recording (peer or adult scribe, IT, pictures)	Visual prompt cards summarising task	Verbal and written structures to support language, e.g. cloze procedures	Structured choices – this and this needs to be done, but student determines	Positive phone call or text to parent(s)/ Carer(s)	Clarify, understand and encourage paraphrasing of instructions	Awareness of writing posture, chair tucked in, 2 feet on floor	Access to alternative means of recording (IT, audio recording)	Repeat core points made by students during class discussion
F	Use of highlighter pen for text work	Peer or small group working	Use of blue tack 'stress ball' to self-occupy	Use of PowerPoint to structure self-presentations	Explicit praise of student to class	Use of rating scale for self-assessment	Provide student with a '?' card, to indicate a request for help	Provide pre-prepared formats of graphs, charts etc	Provision of homework instruction on photocopied sheet	Use of appropriate auxiliary aids

judith.carter@willowtreelearning.co.uk

Class List Identifying Barriers to Learning

judith.carter@willowtreelearning.co.uk

Name of Learner	SEN Support/ EHCP	Literacy	Learning	Listening/ Attention	Speech/ Language	Behaviour/ Control	Confidence/ Emotion	Social Skills/ Comm	Organisation	Physical	Sensory	Support Strategies

Promoting engagement and ownership of SEND by subject teachers in secondary schools can be systemically challenging. This is not because subject teachers are less committed to SEND than their primary colleagues, but instead, often relates to the apparent 'systemic disconnect' that can emerge in secondary schools. This systemic disconnect often relates to the difference in practice and expectation of subject departments and the SEND department. The SENCO and SEND Practitioner may work tirelessly to comply with the SEND system, by producing provision maps and/ or learning programmes that are shared on electronic platforms, but the impact on subject teaching may be minimal or non-existent. It may be difficult for the SENCO or SEND Practitioner to track subject teacher take-up and use of electronic information and resources. Similarly, unless the Senior Leadership Team are actively involved in the monitoring and quality assurance activities relating to SEND, it can be difficult to develop practice and ensure that adjustments, support and interventions are implemented. Often TAs have been relied on to provide in-class support and adjustments for learners in secondary classes, but this is not always available. Secondary SENCOs and SEN Practitioners seeking to plan provision with purpose, are encouraged to attempt to address this disconnect by developing a system that requires greater subject teacher engagement with SEND. For example, identifying a lead SEND link teacher from each subject to liaise with the SENCO on a half termly basis. Or by ensuring that subject leads or heads of department/faculty take on this liaison role. Creating a system that requires regular communication between the SEND team and teachers is the first step to promoting this connection. The focus of the half-termly collaboration could be to share adjustment and support menus with each subject lead and ask them to disseminate this to subject teachers, who in turn will ask them to identify the approaches to be used in their classes. The subject team could also personalise and adapt the content of adjustment and support menus to ensure relevance and adaptation. The SENCO or SEN Practitioner would also be able to share individual student information and outline the purpose of interventions promoting insight into individual learner needs. It is essential that all secondary SENCOs and SEN Practitioners regularly evaluate the effectiveness of their systems in the school and ensure their compliance to the Code of Practice especially in relation to the engagement of subject teachers with learners with SEND. If your current system primarily involves yourself and TAs working in parallel to subject teachers, then continue to strive to bridge this disconnect. Afterall, however effective your practice is, if it is an 'add on' rather than an integrated approach to teaching, your impact will be less than if the two systems connect.

The final resource in this chapter, intended to support you, as you support teachers, is a coaching conversation prompt. This could be used to aid developmental conversations with staff. It can also be a useful structure for supervision and professional reflection.

Coaching Conversation Tool

Introduction
- Agree time available and focus of discussion
- Clarify role of Coach and Coachee – Coach will listen, reflect and explore issues and the Coachee will share experiences and thinking. Together we will consider any collaborative action point(s)

Individual child-focused conversation
- Tell me about this child – family context, friendship, interests
- Strengths and barriers to learning
- What are your concerns?

Action taken and goal setting
- What are you already doing to support access to learning?
- Why are you doing this instead of something else?
- Has it made any difference?
- Why do you think that is?
- What would you like to change for that learner?
- Do they and their parents/carers share this goal?

Achieving this goal
- What are the first steps towards this goal?
- What would the learner need to do to achieve this?
- Who could help them? Family? Friends? School staff?
- How can you facilitate this?
- What might limit the achievement of this?
- What steps could be taken to mitigate this?

Next steps
- Having explored these issues and identified a goal, what can you do tomorrow?
- What support do you need?
- How can you share this suggestion with the learner? Their family? Friends? Staff?
- When shall we review this?

Process review
- How did it feel to engage with this coaching conversation?
- Would you suggest any changes to the structure?
- Has your thinking moved on as a result of this conversation?
- Any questions or comments?
- Thank you for participating

Play and lunchtime supervisors

Play and lunchtime supervisors also have potential to contribute to SEND provision. Their interaction with learners during unstructured times will intentionally or unintentionally impact on their experience of the day. How many times can you recall an incident where a learner left the class before lunch feeling positive and successful, but returned from lunch angry, frustrated or unhappy? Of course, the attribution of this change may not have directly related to staff, but a member of staff is likely to have had contact with the learner at some point in this process. There are so many reasons why a learner may return to class distressed after break or lunchtime, ranging from peer conflict or confusion, sensory overload, communication difficulties, anxiety or even disappointment about the contents of their lunch! The focus here is not on the possible triggers of this change, but the potential actions that may have reduced their impact. What could an adult have done to minimise or mitigate this issue? **With training, awareness and time, play and lunchtime supervisors can offer far more advocacy for learners and have the potential to offer SEND provision in a social context.** But it is essential that they have training and support. Again, you are encouraged to consider your SEND CPD programme and to reflect on the inclusion of play and lunchtime supervisors in training opportunities. Empowering play and lunchtime supervisors to offer positive token rewards to learners engaging in co-operative play or modelling helpful behaviours, can in itself contribute to greater positive interactions. Learners are often aware of the hierarchical status of adults in schools and may deem the lunchtime supervisor to be less significant than their teacher or TA. But by sharing the rewards system or 'currency', and training staff on positive rewarding, their perceived status as potential rewarders gains more equity. Empowering lunchtime supervisors to provide positive feedback cards to teachers can be useful. Some examples are included, but encouraging your learners and staff to design and develop their own system may have the most impact.

The greatest potential of lunchtime supervisors with regards to SEND provision, relates to their capacity to form positive relationships with learners and to engage and model play and social communication skills. Of course, they have a responsibility to monitor the safety of all learners and organise lunch consumption itself, but appointing lunchtime supervisors to co-ordinate peer play leaders or to set up structured play tasks could be a useful addition to the SEND provision offered to some learners. It could also potentially resolve conflict and subsequent emotional dysregulation that can threaten to disrupt post lunchtime learning!

Others

This last group is of course a catchall group for other adults that may visit the school. This might include volunteers, governors, caretaking and administrative staff, community representatives or commissioned external services including Educational Psychologists, Speech, Occupational and Play Therapists as well as counsellors etc. The reason for including them in this chapter is not of course to suggest that they will be directly contributing to the SEND provision offered in the school, but their interactions and attitudes are equally influential as they contribute to the experience of learners. Ensuring that all adults entering the school or setting adopt an inclusive and positive approach to all learners should be encouraged. In the same way as we promote safeguarding as our shared responsibility, so is the promotion of equality and value to all. As an Educational Psychologist myself, I write letters to individual learners that I work with, thanking them for meeting with me and sharing some of the things that I noticed about them as a learner. I do of course write a report for the school and family, but the learner letter often generates as much feedback as the report. The reason for the letter to learners and indeed the rationale for including this here, is that it is an aspect of my practice that reflects my inclusive values and person-centred approach. It is the combination of all of our values and approaches that contribute to your school culture. As such, it is important that these are shared. Booth and Ainscow in the index for inclusion (2011) write:

"Inclusion is most importantly seen as putting inclusive values into action…Values are fundamental guides and prompts to action. They spur us forward, give us a sense of direction and define a destination" (page 21).

All members of your learning community, through their interactions, contribute to the definition of your destination. **As SENCOs or SEN Practitioners, you are leaders who can champion equality of education for all. Remembering that equality is not about treating people in the same way or expecting them to be doing the same thing, but rather, equality is about treating people differently, so they can have the same opportunities. SEND provision is part of this right for difference, in order to access the same opportunity to learn and progress.**

Implications for SENCOs and SEN Practitioners

The actions and attitudes of adults impact on learning, so what we do and how we do it matters! A casual negative comment can contribute to lifelong negative belief. Low aspiration is infectious and poses the threat of fulfilment. Direct or indirect discouragement can disperse interest and belief. As such, we must remain mindful of our comments and interactions with learners, and those of others. The role of adults in a learning community is the ultimate super-power! Their positive belief, aspiration and encouragement can transform lives. As SENCOs and SEN Practitioners, this is even more relevant, as you are working with learners who have already been identified by the system as experiencing risk or disadvantage. It is essential that our engagement is strengths-based and values diversity. The SEND provision that is offered should build skills, strengths and aspirations, and overcome or, where possible, remove barriers to learning. So that every learner maximises their learning and independence and can value their own individual contribution. Planning SEND provision with purpose is ultimately about enabling learners to have the best chance to be and to become themselves.

Reflections

- How engaged are adults in the school community?
- How would you define your culture and values?
- Are there actions that you could take to further develop the contribution of adults to SEND provision?

References

Index for Inclusion: Developing Learning and Participation in Schools (2011). Tony Booth and Mel Ainscow. Bristol: Centre for Studies in Inclusive Education (CSIE).

Life Coaching for Kids: A Practical Manual to Coach Children and Young People to Success, Well-being and Fulfilment (2014) Nikki Giant. London: Jessica Kingsley Publishers.

Mind and Society: The Development of Higher Psychological Processes (1978) Lev Vygotsky. Cambridge, MA: Harvard University Press.

The Psychology of Intelligence (2001) Jean Piaget. London: Routledge.

When the Adults Change Everything Changes: Seismic Shifts in School Behaviour (2017) Paul Dix. Carmarthen: Independent Thinking Press.

Working with Parents to Support Children's Learning: Four Recommendations on Working with Parents to Support their Child's Learning (2018) The Education Endowment Foundation. Available at https://educationendowmentfoundation.org.uk/ (Accessed 1 May 2021).

8. Interventions – to buy or not to buy?

If I were reading this book as a SENCO or SEN Practitioner, instead of writing it, I wonder if this is the chapter I would choose to read first? This is because, for many of us, we often feel such pressure to find *the* intervention that will make the difference for that learner or group of learners. We also feel great responsibility to provide value for money from our purchasers and we want to ensure that we are doing the 'best' for our learners. We may also have a professional 'fear of missing out' (FOMO) reaction, on behalf of our learners. I know I do! The constant 'nagging' thought that everyone else knows something that I don't and, somewhere between completing the day job, balancing family and friends and attempting to take care of myself, I might have 'missed' that vital message! As a result, we search our networks, scan websites, read books and track tweets, in the hope that we will find that one occasion where someone tells us the definitive action we should be taking for learners with SEND.

Alas, this book is not able to do this. Indeed, I would argue that there is not one book or single resource that is able to do this, or perhaps even should? That is because, the needs of every learner, family, teacher, TA, SENCO and SEN Practitioner are individual. In the same way that every required action (or solution) is also individual. Although this may feel a little disappointing, it is in fact good news. It means there is not a single definitive answer that you have missed, in fact quite the opposite! You have all the skills you need to collaborate with others to generate a personalised approach which will move a learner forward, either by attempting to overcome or, if possible, to remove, a barrier to learning that they are currently experiencing. You have those skills now. They are yours. You have not 'missed' *the* message! Disappointingly though, this book is not going to provide you with a list of published resources and encourage you to buy them. (However, there are many wonderful catalogues that will do exactly that.) That said, what the book will do, is explore the process of selecting interventions so that you can decide with confidence whether to buy a resource or indeed to make your own.

Making your own resources or developing your own personalised intervention programmes does not imply less professionalism. It also does not mean that the learner will progress at a lesser rate. Equally, it does not guarantee that the learner

DOI: 10.4324/9781003179436-8

will progress more quickly either. The factors that influence progression are the *relevance* of the action to the learner and their level of *engagement*. In reality, personalised resources can be far more relevant and engaging to a learner than generic or published resources, simply because they have been created with or for that individual. But this does of course take time and demands knowledge of the desired outcome. **Defining the desired outcome or anticipated impact of the intervention, is the key to selecting the appropriate action. It is only by knowing what we want to be different for that learner, that we can begin to consider what actions may achieve this.** It is this information that will help you to decide whether to 'buy or not to buy' an intervention or programme to be used with a learner.

The 7 Cs Learning Portfolio provides a language of assessment, which in turn gives you a consistent language for intervention. By defining the barriers to learning, you are able to aspire with the learner and their parents/carers, to what could be different or developed. The risk is that these aspirations become 'hidden' by the very targets that are written to define them! For example, if the 7 Cs Progress Tracker is used **as** the target, then this will not help to inform the action. If a teacher writes an area for development or target as "to increase working memory from 3 to 5" (referring to the rating scale of 1–9) then this is utterly meaningless. It does not help the learner, their family or themselves to plan actions to take. Instead, if they write "James can now remember one part of an instruction and we want him to remember three parts of an instruction at the end of half term," this in itself tells the learner, their family and the teacher to rehearse the skill of remembering three things. **The relationship teachers, learners, parents and carers have with the wording of targets, is in itself the key to defining the actions to be taken.**

Targeted outcomes

For many years, educationalists, especially in the world of SEND, have focused on targets. We can all recall the importance of creating a SMART target, that is specific, measurable, achievable, relevant and time-related, and most of us can recount this requirement in our sleep! But were we actually very good or even consistent in this? The 2014 revisions to the Code of Practice shifted our focus from targets to outcomes, which had a greater emphasis on the *implication* of the target. A target defines the desired change, but an outcome is intended to define the impact of that change on the learner. For example, a target may have been for a learner to be able to 'write more words', but the outcome would be, 'James will be able to write more words **so he can** write birthday cards to his friends and family.' The shift in focus to the 'so (s)he can…' is really important. And it is this addition that helps to inform the nature of our action or interventions. Perhaps we should no longer think about targets in isolation, but instead focus on capturing *targeted outcomes*?

Working with teachers to develop their skills and capacity with capturing their aspirations for learners with SEND, i.e. writing targeted outcomes, is essential if they are to commission relevant interventions that will promote learner engagement. Of course, the temptation is to start with a list of interventions and select relevant approaches for an individual or group of learners. Indeed, this may have been your expectation or indeed hope of this chapter, in which case I am sorry to disappoint. But instead of starting with the list of interventions, define the targeted outcome which will in itself define the action that is required. This is illustrated on the 7 Cs targeted outcome grids that follow. When you read the targeted outcomes, consider what actions could prompt, rehearse or lead to the achievement of this, and that becomes the personalised intervention for that learner. Also please keep in mind that these examples are generic in nature. I am attempting to illustrate a starting point that may be relevant for a 5-year-old or a 15-year-old! As you read the examples, consider how you could adapt the wording for particular learners and ensure that the targeted outcomes are specific, measurable, achievable, relevant to that learner and time-related. A good tip is to define what will be achieved, why this is useful for the learner and when it will be achieved by. The examples offered in the grids are starting points and should not be viewed as fully completed or personalised SMART targeted outcomes.

7 Cs Learning Portfolio – Sample of Targeted Outcomes

Cognition	Targeted Outcomes	Relevant and Engaging Action Ideas
Working Memory	• Jane will remember 3 parts of an instruction **so she can** follow requests in school and at home. • James will use post its to write down 2 things he needs to do when he goes upstairs **so he can** remember.	• Playing memory games, rehearsing 3 elements, saying aloud and prompting with her fingers. • Word association games – identify 1 key word to aid memory recall and write it down.
Speed of Processing	• Oliver will increase his reaction times when playing games, **so he** is able to respond more quickly. • Jemima will identify key words in instructions, say them aloud and explain what they mean to her **so she can** understand.	• Play snap, whack a mole, Buckaroo, hungry hippo type games. • Adults will repeat key instructions to Jemima and ask her paraphrase to identifying the key words that help her understanding.
Inference	• Louise will listen to instructions and summarise what she perceives are the implied actions she has to take and share this with her friend **so she can** understand. • When reading, Steven will pause to ask and answer questions about the text, **so he can** think more about the story greater thought and interest in the book.	• Adults will give Louise key instructions and she will then share the implications of this with her friend. The adult will check out their understanding. • Adults reading with Steven will model asking him questions and encourage him to answer and in time, to identify his own questions.
Anticipation	• Before asking for help, Andrew will stop and think about what he might need to do next, which he can share with a friend or adult, **so he can** have greater understanding. • Annie will consider possible implications of actions arising from shared social scenarios and discuss these with others, **so she can** start to think about her actions.	• When Andrew thinks he has finished a task or when he is about to start the task, he will stop and tell his friend what he thinks he has to do next. • In pairs or small groups, share social scenarios and ask a range of 'what if' type questions to help explore actions and consequences.

Cognition	Targeted Outcomes	Relevant and Engaging Action Ideas
Reflection	• Imran will reflect over the events in his day and identify two positives and share why he thinks these were positive, **so he** is able to 'notice' future success. • Chloe will explain what she has learnt and when she might be able to use this again, after each science lesson, **so she can** notice her developing skills.	• For 2 weeks encourage Imran to use a written diary, voice recorder or a video diary to capture two positives in every day. • At the end of science, an adult will ask Chloe to summarise her perceived learning and the relevance of this, recording when it might be useful again.
Evaluation	• Jasmine will present an argument in favour or against a topic of her choosing, having researched the topic, demonstrating how she has weighed up the information **so she can** demonstrate. • Lavislav will write a 'so what do I think' paragraph at the end of his homework where he can synthesise information and make his own conclusion, **so he** is able to trust his own future ideas.	• Jasmine will engage in a project of interest, researching information using varied sources and then make a written or video recorded evaluation of what she has found to share with peers. • Lavislav will create his own written, voice or video record of his thoughts regarding the skills or information he has taken from his homework.
Analysis	• Sumi will identify the similarities and differences between two sources of information **so she can** provide a written account of these, to aid her understanding. • Chris will review the work of some of his peers and consider their work against the specified instructions, identifying similarities, **so he can** start to focus on details in his own work.	• Using a question prompt, Sumi will identify similarities and differences from two sources and write these as a list. • Using clear marking criteria, Chris will look at the work of some of his peers and rank them in order of accuracy against the criteria.

7 Cs Learning Portfolio – Sample of Targeted Outcomes

Communication	Targeted Outcomes	Relevant and Engaging Action Ideas
Expressive Vocabulary	• Ritchie will increase the number of category words that he knows **so he can** use these to help him organise and recall words in speech and writing. • Sarah will be able to choose between 8 emotion words **so she can** describe her feelings at home and at school.	• Using object photo cards, Joshua will sort the photos into relevant categories. He will also create his own category word folder with words and pictures. • Using emojis as prompts, Sarah will be taught the feelings words and match them to her own experiences.
Articulation	• Roopa will be able to say the p and s sounds with accuracy and fluency when talking, **so she can** share her thoughts more clearly. • Joshua will feel more confident to say words with the 'oo' and 'ee' sound **so he can** share more of his ideas.	• Play vocalisation games, sing rhymes and rehearse saying words in play. • Use microphone, echo games, songs and rhymes to rehearse sounds. Play imitation games with puppets.
Language and Comprehension	• Bina will increase her understanding of curriculum subject words, **so she** is able to follow instructions. • Tim will increase the number of positioning words he knows, **so he can** have greater understanding and follow instructions.	• Pre-teach subject and topic words explicitly describing their meaning and creating a visual prompt or association. • Explicitly teach position words including, on, in, under, over, inside, outside and rehearse these via role play.
Collaborative Conversation	• Ashwin will participate in a two way conversation with a peer making up to 3 comments, **so he** is able to listen and adapt his own words in response to the comments of others. • Jo will ask questions of peers to initiate a conversation and share 2 verbal exchanges **so she can** increase her confidence.	• Provide opportunities for Ashwin and peers to role play characters and or to talk about topics of interest. • Rehearse conversation starters with Jo and ask her to choose two favourites that she can then try to use with peers during playtime.

Communication	Targeted Outcomes	Relevant and Engaging Action Ideas
Listening	• Colin will answer questions when he is reading, **so he can** demonstrate his effective listening skills following an extract of a story. • Suzette will follow the actions integrated into a series of instructions, **so she can** demonstrate her effective listening skills.	• Use reading comprehension cards or extracts of story books with Colin and then ask relevant questions about what he has heard. • Play 'Simon says' type games where instructions are given for actions.
Social Communication (output)	• Angie will use an ice-breaker to start a conversation with peers during lunchtime, **so she can** feel more confident when sitting with new people. • George will identify his preferred 'greeting' to use when meeting new people at home or at school, **so he can** feel more confident.	• Explicitly teach a range of ice-breakers, such as 'how was your morning? Did you have a good morning? How are you today? Are you hungry?' and rehearse their application. • Explicitly teach and rehearse a range of greetings that George could use in different contexts.
Social Interaction (input)	• Kylie will be able to answer a question asked by peers **so she can** feel more confident in her response. • Jamie will be able to apply 'holding' comments to questions if he does not understand or know the answer **so he can** increase his confidence with uncertainty.	• Using role play and rehearsal, explicitly teach how to use the question to structure the answer. E.g., How are you? Thank you for asking how I am, I am fine. • Explicitly teach a sample of 'holding' responses such as, 'I will let you know,' 'oh really, interesting,' or 'ok then.'

7 Cs Learning Portfolio – Sample of Targeted Outcomes

Creativity	Targeted Outcomes	Relevant and Engaging Action Ideas
Generation of Ideas	• Tom will generate the end of a story during his weekly group **so he** feels more confident to share his ideas. • Eve will suggest a game the family can play during the weekend **so she can** enjoy sharing her ideas.	• Set up a small story telling group who share a bag of 'props' and each create part of the narrative. • Structured ideas for games can be presented at the start but the learner is then encouraged to adapt ideas.
Problem-solving	• Rowan will select the next step when presented with weekly social scenarios to resolve, **so she can** feel more confident. • Tobias will solve a weekly mystery game on the iPad identifying the actions taken to reach the conclusion **so he can** show how he reached this solution.	• Create a set of social scenario cards to share with a 'solving circle.' Use extracts from films, YouTube clips or soaps to prompt discussion. • Download suitable mystery games onto an electronic tablet.
Attention	• Kirstie will focus for 10 minutes on the carpet and summarise key points **so she** gains greater experience of understanding information. • David will increase his accuracy and fluency with noticing visual information **so he can** aid his focus when working.	• Adults will ask learner to paraphrase work instructions. They will rehearse skills using reading comprehension tasks verbally, explicitly pointing out key words • Play spot the difference tasks, missing objects and dot-to-dot activities.
Motivation	• Jacinda will set her own weekly goal for maths and describe what she has to do to achieve this **so she can** celebrate her success at the end of the week. • Karl will select his own 'next' activities (as part of the now and next work structure) **so he** feels encouraged to complete the now task.	• Adults engage with coaching conversations to encourage learner identification of goal-setting and protect time to review and celebrate success. • Create a list of favourite activities so the learner can select from the list to help motivate and sustain effort.

Creativity	Targeted Outcomes	Relevant and Engaging Action Ideas
Making Things	• Phoebe will host a craft group with 3 other children where they will develop a shared 'creation' to show the class each week, **so she can** gain confidence and experience. • Zac to increase accuracy with following a recipe **so he can** plan and make his own healthy snack.	• Provide a box of junk modelling resources, fabrics, paints, pencils etc and a set of cards with theme ideas. Encourage the group to discuss and agree their ideas. • Use cookbooks or websites to find relevant recipes and ask learner to generate a shopping list for ingredients.
Courage and Determination	• Sara will attempt a new challenge every Saturday at home, working with her Mum **so she can** experience success. • Harrison will use his 5 lives cards to have a go at answering questions that he feels unsure about, **so he can** see that mistakes are part of learning.	• Staff to work with family to identify a 'challenge' list for learner to engage with. Include physical, agility, cognitive, communication and creative challenges. • Teacher learner to use the 5 fingers on their hand to indicate 'lives' or attempts to use when working. Discuss the courage it takes to make a mistake.
Trust	• Andrea will work with a partner to complete trust games where they each take a turn to 'lead' the other person, **so she can** experience trusting someone and being trusted. • George to take the lead in a group activity **so he can** experiences others trusting him.	• Develop a menu of trust games, e.g. follow my lead, what's in the box and can you tell what it is? Encourage group to engage in tasks and talk about experiences and feelings. • Provide opportunities for learner to lead others and discuss how it feels when others trust you.

7 Cs Learning Portfolio – Sample of Targeted Outcomes

Control	Targeted Outcomes	Relevant and Engaging Action Ideas
Self-regulation	• Amy will use her exit card to indicate the need to retreat to her safe space during lesson times, **so she** is able to take time out for self-regulation. • Ezra will write down his immediate thought rather than seeking to tell the teacher straight away and later organise three thoughts he wants to share, **so he** starts to regulate his ideas.	• Agree with the learner how and when an exit card can be used and where the learner's safe place is. Provide chosen activities, e.g. book, Lego for use in safe space and a timer so they know to return after an agreed time limit. • Provide a thought journal so key words can be written down instead of shouted out.
Behaviour for Learning	• Victoria will manage her own workspace ensuring that she has the right equipment for each lesson, **so she** is able to begin work tasks on request. • James will use a mind map to help capture his ideas **so he** is able to organise his work independently	• Create a work station checklist detailing equipment and expectations for use. • Teach learner how to use mind mapping as a way for capturing ideas. Provide opportunities for rehearsal of skills.
Anxiety Management	• Julie will write down any anxious thoughts she has in her worry book **so she can** talk about these with Mr Jones and identify actions she could take, increasing her confidence to cope. • Stefan will identify a range of thinking bias examples given to his group and asked to notice any he sees in himself, **so he** is more able to recognise his own thought patterns.	• Learner to have own worry book to record concerns. These can be shared in a weekly meeting with a familiar member of staff who can talk about actions that may mitigate the concerns. • Create thinking bias scenario statements such as "everyone hates me" and encourage learners to sort them into groups.

Control	Targeted Outcomes	Relevant and Engaging Action Ideas
Confidence	• Eliza will say to herself "I can do this" at the start of an activity, **so she can** remind herself that she believes in herself. • Jeremy will practice using subject words before the lesson, **so he can** feel more familiar with the words and he can help others, increasing his belief in his capacity.	• Individually or in a small group teach self-affirmation and encourage learners to identify a preferred statement that they can say to themselves to boost their self-belief and confidence. • In small groups use pre-teaching to expose learners to new vocab so they may have greater understanding in the lesson.
Resilience	• Zara will identify positive comments about herself during her Friday Reflection meeting with Mrs Baker **so she can** start to notice her strengths. • William will choose between an easy or hard task at the end of Maths **so he can** safely experience success and possible failure, boosting his ability to cope.	• Small group discussion where learners identify positive attributes about themselves and give and receive compliments. Discuss what these attributes help with. • Develop a set of challenge cards with short activities that will lead to success.
Language of Emotions	• Fatima will use emoji cards and words to indicate her feelings during the day at school, **so she** is able to describe her feelings in words. • Simon will use an emotions thermometer to help express his feelings and to notice any changes, **so he** feels more able to identify feelings.	• Encourage the learner to create a personalised set of emoji cards with words and pictures to indicated feelings. Keep them on the desk for self-monitoring. • Describe emotions and triggers that cause changes. Present these on a thermometer and encourage independent monitoring and expression of feelings.
Independence	• Lucy to use her 'now and next' board to determine what her next action should be without asking for help, **so she** is able to gain confidence by herself. • Philip will complete tasks from his activity box working alone, for 20 mins every day, **so he can** gain positive experiences of self-direction.	• Explicitly teach the use of a now and next timetable, providing a resource box of independent 'next' activities. • Develop a personalised box of activities such as jigsaw, spot the difference, Lego model, colour by number etc and teach independent application.

7 Cs Learning Portfolio – Sample of Targeted Outcomes

Compassion	Targeted Outcomes	Relevant and Engaging Action Ideas
Friendships	• Carmel will play with her circle of friends during 3 breaktimes each week, **so she can** experience shared play. • Alex will join the play leader scheme and help younger children to play games at lunchtime **so he** gains confidence with others.	• Establish a circle of friends for and with a learner and provide support to the circle. • At a whole school level set up a play leader scheme where learners can offer support to younger children whilst continuing to experience play opportunities.
Turn-taking	• Shungu will play board games with another child during two lunchtimes a week, **so she can** rehearse turn-taking skills. • Davy to attend the handbell ringing lunchtime club **so he can** participate in regular turn-taking activities.	• Provide a range of board games that can be completed within 20 minutes. Teach rules and turn-taking. • Organise any group activity such as a music or games club where turn-taking is an essential requirement. Link to learner interests.
Empathy	• Lizzie to take part in a weekly small group discussion exploring actions and consequences, **so she can** gain experience of another perspective. • Claude will name the emotions that he thinks would be felt by different story characters when listening to a story each week, **so he can** think about other people's feelings.	• Develop a series of social scenarios or stories that can be told from different perspectives. Encourage small group discussion and reflection. • Provide emotion cards and prompts that can be shared when listening to stories or scenarios. Discuss in a small group.
Sense of Justice	• Jenny will try to explain why she thinks something is 'unfair' and suggest a positive alternative, **so she** gains experience with communicating her thoughts. • Benoit will use a restorative approach to help manage conflict with peers **so he can** help to promote shared understanding of incidents.	• Use circle time to create a culture of discussion and reflection on topics such as fairness and justice. • Encourage learners to explain why something is either fair or unfair. • Explicitly teach restorative approaches to managing conflict and enable learners to rehearse these skills.

Compassion	Targeted Outcomes	Relevant and Engaging Action Ideas
Self-esteem	• Leanne will identify a positive action or incident from each day, identifying her contribution to this **so she can** start to see her worth. • Zak will work with a small circle of friends to give and receive compliments **so he can** listen to how others view him.	• Provide learners with a celebration journal or scrapbook where they can capture positives as they occur in the day. • Teach learners how to give and receive compliments, linking to people's actions and strengths.
Self-efficacy	• Ruth will choose how to present her work during a lesson every day, **so she** gains experience of decision making and expressing her choice. • Graham will keep a weekly scrapbook that captures all activities or actions taken where he 'made a difference,' **so he can** start to see his own potential.	• Ensure that learners have options regarding presentation, e.g. writing in pen or pencil, typing, voice recording or working with a peer scribe. • Individual learner scrapbooks or workbooks to create a record of achievements.
Support for Others	• Marian will play structured games within her peer pyramid during 3 lunchtimes a week, **so she is** able to gain experience of social play. • Edward to host a gaming group two lunchtimes a week, **so he** is able to engage in shared activities with others.	• Identify 2 peers to participate with the learner in a 'peer pyramid' and teach a variety of games. • Nominate key lunchtime staff to 'look out' for positive play. • Encourage the learner to share an interest or skill and establish a lunchtime group.

7 Cs Learning Portfolio – Sample of Targeted Outcomes

Co-ordination	Targeted Outcomes	Relevant and Engaging Action Ideas
Fine Motor Skills	• Marie will increase accuracy and fluency with writing vertical, horizontal and circular movements three times a week, **so she** is able to write letters with greater control. • Bobby will increase accuracy and fluency with cutting with scissors **so he** is able to cut out his work neatly.	• Provide templates for copying vertical, horizontal and circular shapes in isolation, vary size and encourage transfer to letter formation. • Provide a range of tasks involving cutting, e.g., making snowflakes, cutting paper for chains, cutting spirals etc.
Gross Motor Skills	• Leah will throw and catch a ball during ball skills group three lunchtimes a week, **so she** has more confidence and accuracy. • Alistair will complete an obstacle course with 2 peers during 3 lunchtimes a week, **so he** gains fluency and balance with movements.	• Provide a variety of equipment, e.g. football, tennis ball, balloon etc for use by the group. Teach skills in isolation and allow learners to play with throwing and catching. • Create simple obstacle course in the playground and promote participation and exploration.
Sensory	• Katie will evaluate whether the sound field helps her to access teacher instructions and share her experiences with staff, **so she** gains confidence in expressing her views and is able to request changes. • Daniel will paraphrase work instructions at the start of every session **so he can** check out his understanding of expectations.	• Adults to wear sound field microphones when talking to the class and to meet with individual learners to check out their access to information. • Staff to ask learner to recap key information and demonstrate their understanding of work requirements.
Mobility	• Alison will use her wheelchair for play and lunchtimes but will vary posture between sitting and standing during lessons, accessing an adjustable desk **so she can** increase her stability and stretch her back. • Kenny will complete his core muscle workout programme three times a week, **so he can** develop greater strength and posture control.	• Access to a variety of equipment including a height adjustable desk and or standing frame. • Personalised programme from a Physio or Occupational Therapist with access to appropriate equipment and resources.

(Continued)

191

Co-ordination	Targeted Outcomes	Relevant and Engaging Action Ideas
Stability and Balance	• Bryony will balance on the wobble board for 6 minutes retaining accuracy and control over her movements, **so she can** feel more stable when walking around the class. • Devi will develop greater fluency and accuracy to hop, stand, jump and walk along a line, so **she is** able to move with greater confidence at playtime.	• Access to a wobble board. • Personalised programme of activities to be delivered 3 times a week during lunchtimes and as part of PE warm-up activities.
Posture	• Lisa will choose how to work during afternoon sessions, opting to sit, stand or lay on the floor, **so she can** vary her posture and express her preferences. • Damien will work on a gym ball during maths lessons in the morning and immediately after lunch break, **so he can** vary and aid his posture.	• Ensure access to a standing desk, chair and clipboard and cushion to ensure a variety of posture options. • Provide a workspace that includes a chair and a gym ball, so posture options can be exchanged.
Sensory Processing	• Gloria will choose when to wear headphones to help screen out additional sounds, **so she is** able to manage her own sensory experiences. • Manny will complete his sensory activities three times a week, **so he can** increase his experience of sounds and touch.	• Access to headphones or ear defenders to be worn when useful. • Personalised sensory programme including sound activities and touch, such as sand and water play.

7 Cs Learning Portfolio – Sample of Targeted Outcomes

Curriculum	Targeted Outcomes	Relevant and Engaging Action Ideas
English	• Hayley will build CVC words daily using the identified 18 letter sounds **so she can** use these words in reading and writing. • Dylan will use a voice recorder three times a week, to say his sentences prior to writing them, **so he is** able to remember his ideas.	• Create a sheet containing the 18 sounds randomly presented and encourage the learner to put sounds together to build words. • Explicitly teach how to use a voice recorder and playback recordings to aid writing.
Maths	• Beatrice will rehearse number bonds to 20 daily and be able to recite these fluently **so she can** complete simple mental calculations. • Jay will rehearse o'clock, half past, quarter past and quarter to daily, using digital and analogue methods **so he can** use his watch independently.	• Play number games, e.g. adding dice, dominoes, and using Numicon to gain fluency with numbers. • Access to digital clocks and analogue faces to rehearse the connection between the number of minutes in an hour.
Science	• Penny will identify similarities between minibeasts, identifying 6 familiar types **so she can** find an name these in her garden by half term. • Raj will create his own weather record over 4 weeks and identify patterns and frequency of weather types, **so he** is able to describe the top 3 most occurring weather types.	• Access to minibeast reference materials, to be used to create her own models and pictures of common types. • Access to an outdoor thermometer, weather chart and weather app for recording information.
Art and Music	• Monica will use drawing, sculpture and painting to replicate works by the artist Kandinsky, **so she** gains confidence in using materials for herself. • Joey will listen to types of music genre and identify similarities and differences between styles, **so he** is able to label types of music he hears.	• Access to a variety of visual images and studies of Kandinsky's work as well as a range of practical materials for independent use and exploration. • Access to music and musical instruments. Small group discussion of sounds and use of a checklist to identify sounds.

Curriculum	Targeted Outcomes	Relevant and Engaging Action Ideas
History and Geography	• Chantel will create her own family tree, identifying her place within it, **so she** has a greater understanding of her family and the concept of the past. • Ross will use a map of the school to identify his location and move between sites, **so he** is able to plan a route between classrooms in high school.	• Family tree examples, e.g. the royal family and famous celebrity or fictional families can be used to help the learner visualise and develop their own tree. • Access to own school map and high school map.
Computing	• Dot will use an online search engine to find information relating to her interests, twice a week, **so she** gains confidence with locating and extracting relevant points. • Leonard will use coding to direct a robot through a simple maze, **so he** gains confidence and fluency with coding language and skills.	• Secure internet access and time to explore a variety of sources linked to an agreed theme or project. • Working individually or in pairs, learners can code the robot and navigate an agreed route.
PE and Sport	• Ivy will rehearse individual soccer skills **so she can** apply these when playing a team game. • Ted will develop his own warm-up and fitness programme for daily use and record his own times, **so he** feels more confident about physical activity.	• Access to a football skills programme, equipment and coaching. • Watch YouTube exercises to identify types and functions, in order to select a varied programme.

Gathering information

In addition to considering the targeted outcome itself, it may also be useful to consider *how* information is gathered to inform our actions and interventions. Of course, the 7 Cs Learning Portfolio has the potential to extend our shared language of assessment and curriculum attainment data reveals the application of skills in curriculum subjects. But how can we gather information to inform interventions linked to other areas of need? The ultimate 'tool' in the toolkit of a SENCO and or SEN Practitioner is the skill of consultation. Skilfully eliciting the views of learners, parents/carers, teachers and TAs around next steps is essential. The process itself can then help to identify the need and nature of any adjustments, support or interventions. Asking relevant questions and triangulating information is essential. The behaviour analysis grid that follows, is offered as a starting point to help SENCOs and SEN Practitioners to gather information that may help to develop a shared hypothesis about what a learner may be trying to communicate with the presentation of behaviour that is challenging to us or deemed to be complex. The structured information gathering tool encourages shared reflection and a focus on the possible reasons for the behaviour. This in turn leads to the identification of action that can be taken at school and at home. The RRRRRR sheets contain six key actions beginning with 'r' that may help us to identify actions to overcome and remove the barriers associated with the expression of behaviour that challenges us or is complex.

Behaviour Analysis Grid

Learner Name: **Year Group:**   **Date of completion:**

Completed by:

Concern	In school	At home	When out and about
What are the behaviours of concern? (*What do you actually see?*)			
What are the triggers of this behaviour? (*What happens just before this behaviour?*)			
How do adults and peers respond to this behaviour (*What is the reaction of others?*)			
What regulates the learner's behaviour and calms them? (*What do you/they do to recover?*)			
What are the perceived motives for this behaviour? (*What does the learner 'get' from this action?*)			
How does the learner respond after an incident? (*Do they appear remorseful, in denial or indifferent?*)			

Action Planning

From the information collected, we agree that the priority needs are:

To try to 'overcome' this barrier we will:

At school:

At home:

To try to 'remove' the barrier we will:

At school:

At home:

We will seek additional information or advice from:

We will meet again to review these concerns on:

The RRRRRR sheet for *Overcoming Behaviour Barriers* (when the learner has lost regulation)

Redirection Provide positive distraction or attention shift	**Retreat** Ensure the learner can choose to retreat to a safe space	**Reconfigure** Where possible change the sensory experience, offering headphones, sunglasses or a sheltered space
Reassure Positive labelling of feelings and relate these to actions that may help	**Remind** Refer to prior experiences and actions the learner tool to help regulate and focus	**Relate** Show empathy and compassion

The RRRRRR sheet for *Removing* Behaviour Barriers (only when the learner is regulated)

Regulate	Re-train	Resolve
Provided opportunities for learners to rehearse controlling emotions, words and actions	Rehearse alternative responses that may replace	Teach how to identify own solutions and positive actions to manage conflict and fear
Rehearse	Realise	Reflect
Try and try again	Present a positive aspiration or version of themselves so the learner can realise this	Encourage consideration and discussion of actions

Sources of intervention ideas

This chapter would not be complete without consideration of the incredible sources of information that exist to help you prioritise interventions either to buy or to develop. The Education Endowment Foundation is of course top of this list of resources, along with the 'What Works' series of websites and resources. Similarly, familiarising yourself with product and publisher catalogues is useful, as you can track resource development and where budgets allow, prioritise spending. It is essential to regularly audit the interventions that you have available, as part of your provision mapping process and the intervention index (Chapter 1) can be a useful tool to aid this. Ensuring that you have some key interventions linked to a range of barriers to learning across all categories of SEND will provide you with a strong foundation. Consider joining national and local SENCO networks, such as nasen, whole school SEND, SEN forum, SENCO Facebook pages and our Willow Tree Learning Essential SENCO Network and/or Forum, as this can provide a useful platform to ask questions and gather other people's views and experiences with interventions. If you are part of a Multi Academy Trust you may well have access to a professional SENCO group and you could create a shared intervention index which will add a depth and variety of intervention ideas. **As always, keep in mind that interventions have a direct link with CPD, both for teachers, TAs and yourselves.** Interventions are, after all, explicit actions of intent which are targeted to facilitate learning, or put simply, a further example of a teaching modality. If you or another colleague are unsure about how best to teach a particular skill, work together to research this, seek advice and enhance your own learning of the subject. Which is, of course, at the heart of CPD. **Remember, with regards to SEND provision, it is not *what* you do or even *how* you do it that matters (although they are of course relevant); the essential question is *why* you are doing this.**

Useful Websites: Cognition and Learning

Barriers to Learning	Websites
Literacy	http://www.thedyslexia-spldtrust.org.uk/ https://www.bdadyslexia.org.uk/
Maths	https://www.nationalnumeracy.org.uk/helping-children-maths https://www.twinkl.co.uk/search?term=max%27s%20marvellous%20maths
Memory	https://www.academia.edu/2651164/Working_Memory_and_Learning_A_Practical_Guide_for_Teachers_By_Susan_E_Gathercole_and_Tracy_Packiam_Alloway?auto=download https://www.twinkl.co.uk/resources/extra-subjects-parents/parents-activites-games/memory-games-games-and-activities-games-activities-and-crafts-parents
Speed of Processing	https://www.readandspell.com/what-is-processing-speed https://senmagazine.co.uk/behavioural-emotional-and-social-difficulties-besd/11926/supporting-children-with-processing-issues/
Executive Functioning	https://www.psychologytoday.com/gb/basics/executive-function https://childmind.org/article/helping-kids-who-struggle-with-executive-functions/
Inference	https://www.literacyideas.com/teaching-inference https://www.twinkl.co.uk/teaching-wiki/inference

Useful Websites: Communication & Interaction

Barriers to Learning	Websites
Speech	https://ican.org.uk/i-cans-talking-point/parents/ages-and-stages/ https://chatterpack.net/blogs/blog/list-of-free-speech-language-communication-and-send-resources-for-schools-and-parent-carers
Language	https://ican.org.uk/ https://eput.nhs.uk/our-services/essex/south-east-essex-community-health-services/childrens/speech-language-therapy/resources/downloadable-resources/
Social Communication & Interaction	https://www.autismeducationtrust.org.uk/ https://www.autism.org.uk/
Conversation	https://www.educationworks.org.uk/resources/free-resources-from-education-works https://www.understood.org/en/friends-feelings/common-challenges/picking-up-on-social-cues/4-parts-of-a-conversation-how-to-help-kids-with-social-skills-issues-navigate
Listening	https://busyteacher.org/14411-how-to-teach-listening-skills-best-practices.html https://www.eslkidstuff.com/blog/top-10-lists/top-10-listening-activities-without-a-cd
Attention	https://treetopsschool.org/wp-content/uploads/2020/03/Attention-Autism-activity-ideas-sheet.pdf https://www.adhdcare.co.uk/?p=online.resources

Useful Websites: Social, Emotional & Mental Health

Barriers to Learning	Websites
Anxiety	https://youngminds.org.uk/find-help/conditions/anxiety/ https://www.healthcentral.com/article/20-classroom-interventions-for-children-with-anxiety-disorders
Insecure Attachment	https://www.mentallyhealthyschools.org.uk/mental-health-needs/attachment-and-child-development/ https://www.therapistaid.com/therapy-worksheets/cbt/children
Anger	https://www.therapistaid.com/therapy-worksheets/anger/children https://nurtureandthriveblog.com/how-to-teach-your-child-self-regulation/
Resilience	https://youngminds.org.uk/media/1486/interactive_resilience_framework-002.pdf https://cpdonline.co.uk/knowledge-base/safeguarding/building-resilience-in-the-classroom/
Self-esteem	https://positivepsychology.com/self-esteem-for-children/ https://www.justonenorfolk.nhs.uk/emotional-health/children-young-peoples-emotional-health/emotional-health-activities/self-confidence-self-esteem-activities
Friendships	https://www.mentallyhealthyschools.org.uk/media/1901/anti-bullying-toolkit.pdf https://www.bbc.co.uk/cbeebies/grownups/help-your-child-make-friends-at-primary-school

Useful Websites: Physical and Sensory

Barriers to Learning	Websites
Hearing Impairment	https://www.ndcs.org.uk/information-and-support/being-deaf-friendly/information-for-professionals/primary-education/ https://www.natsip.org.uk/doc-library-login/suporting-the-si-workforce/supporting-the-achievement-of-deaf-children-in
Visual Impairment	https://www.rnib.org.uk/services-we-offer-advice-professionals/education-professionals https://www.moorfields.nhs.uk/sites/default/files/Information%20for%20children%20and%20young%20people%20with%20sight%20loss%20and%20their%20families.pdf
Multi-sensory Impairment	https://www.natsip.org.uk/getting-started https://councilfordisabledchildren.org.uk/sites/default/files/field/attachemnt/earlysupportmulti-sensoryimpairmentsfinal2.pdf
Sensory Processing	https://childmind.org/article/how-sensory-processing-issues-affect-kids-in-school/ https://www.boredteachers.com/classroom-management/10-ways-teachers-can-support-students-with-sensory-processing-disorder
Fine Motor Skills	https://www.learning4kids.net/play-by-skills/motor-skills/list-of-fine-motor-play-activities/ https://www.iow.nhs.uk/our-services/community-services/occupational-therapy/Paediatric%20occupational-therapy/Handwriting%20and%20Fine%20motor%20skills
Gross Motor Skills	https://www.yourtherapysource.com/blog1/2020/03/23/gross-motor-skills-and-activities/ https://www.swft.nhs.uk/application/files/6714/5995/2571/gross_motor_skills.pdf

Implications for SENCOs and SEN Practitioners

As a starting point, audit the interventions that you currently provide as part of your SEND provision offer. Link each intervention to its rationale for application, i.e., what barrier to learning is it attempting to overcome? Frequently colleagues 'notice' that there may be a large number of interventions that relate to reading and spelling and perhaps fewer that link to speech, language, social communication and social, emotional and mental health. **It is likely that our curriculum 'bias' has impacted on our selection and purchase of interventions. If we only use the curriculum to assess and define barriers to learning, we will only identify curriculum interventions. This is why the 7 Cs Learning Profile was developed.** Of course, accessing the curriculum remains an entitlement for every learner, including those with SEN, but for those with SEN they are entitled to provision that is 'additional to or different from' that made readily available to others of the same age – so their SEN provision needs to be in addition to the differentiated curriculum offer. It is extra, not instead of, but the provision and intervention that forms your SEND provision should relate to barriers to learning and skills that exceed curriculum subjects.

Reflections

- How diverse is our current range of SEND interventions?
- Do our interventions 'match' the needs of our current learners or are their gaps?
- How do I find out about intervention options? Do I have effective networks of support or is this something I could develop further?

References

The Education Endowment Foundation Teaching and Learning Toolkit (2020) Available at https:// educationendowmentfoundation.org.uk/ (Accessed 1 May 2021).

9. Capturing the impact of SEND provision

Our focus throughout the book has been upon defining and refining the actions with intent, that you offer for learners with SEND. We are aware that SEND provision involves adjustments or teacher tweaks, resources and support, including targeted support from additional adults and of course the interventions that are provided to overcome or remove barriers to learning. We have explored ways of *capturing* your SEND provision and will now consider how you can demonstrate its impact.

Capturing impact is far easier when you have a record of your anticipated impact and or starting point. After all, you then have a benchmark to refer to as you collate information to show the actual impact. This will, of course, often relate to pupil progress towards the targeted outcomes identified at the start of the intervention, or whether the learner has been able to access the learning task because of the adjustments made or support offered. Capturing the overall impact of SEND provision at a strategic level can be more challenging, although if similar methods are applied this can be resolved in the same way. By ensuring that the purpose and anticipated impact of your SEND provision is defined, you will be able to evaluate the actual impact. **It is this process of evaluation that is essential in demonstrating the effectiveness of your provision. So often, SENCOs and SEN Practitioners, alongside teachers and TAs, will record individual learner information regarding what intervention was offered and the individual learner progress. However, we may not always bring this information together and *evaluate* this from a strategic perspective.** The SEND intervention termly evaluation grid may help you to capture your reflections, which can then be summarised for the year and uploaded to your SEN information report and/or shared with senior leaders and governors.

DOI: 10.4324/9781003179436-9

SEND Intervention Evaluation – Term:

Cognition & Learning

Name of Intervention	Number of Learner Participants	Impact	Comments
Memory group – pairs, verbal recall games twice weekly Year 1 and Year 3	8	Teachers report 6/8 responding well with 4/8 presenting with greater confidence and recall in class.	Useful, likely to use again.
Quick Fire games weekly – small group play reaction time games: snap, word association, select and sort – Year 3, 4, 5 and 6	20	Teachers report 14/20 more confident and enjoying games. 4/20 report to feel pressure, 2/20 have had mixed attendance.	Popular with many but not suitable for learners with low confidence.
Spot the difference, can you find group games twice weekly Years 1 and 2	12	Teachers report 12/12 enjoyed the activity. 8/12 appear more alert and focused. 4/12 no visible impact as yet.	Learners like the activities and has good impact for many.
Decoding group – weekly rehearsal of reading skills Year 4	6	Teachers report 5/6 appear more fluent, 4/6 have improved accuracy, remain concerned about 2/6.	Useful and led to improvements.
Read for meaning – weekly comprehension Year 5	8	Teachers report 7/8 actively participated in sessions. 4/8 appear to use greater vocab in writing. Concerned about 1/8 as absent and less motivated.	Well-received by learners. Need to follow up on attendance of 1 learner.
Fine motor control group – twice weekly Year 1	5	Teachers report that 4/5 enjoyed the activities, 1/5 became distressed as unable to complete and became frustrated.	Popular with most learners but those with fear of failure may need more support.
Vocabulary for writing group weekly Year 3	6	Teachers report 6/6 participated and found it helped them plan their writing.	Great intervention, popular and had positive impact on all.
Forwards and backwards – twice weekly counting group Year 2	6	Teachers report 4/6 appear more fluent with greater accuracy. 2/6 remain uncertain, may need more assessment.	Generally useful need to complete additional assessment for 2 learners.
4 Functions – weekly small group rehearsing skills Years 4 and 5	14	Teachers report that 10/14 more confident with greater fluency. Remaining 4/14 still lack independent application. Additional sessions required.	Well-received by most learners – additional assessment could be useful for remaining 4 learners.

SEND Intervention Evaluation – Term:

Cognition & Learning

Name of Intervention	Number of Learner Participants	Impact	Comments

SEND Intervention Evaluation – Term:

Communication & Interaction

Name of Intervention	Number of Learner Participants	Impact	Comments

SEND Intervention Evaluation – Term:
Social, Emotional & Mental Health

Name of Intervention	Number of Learner Participants	Impact	Comments

SEND Intervention Evaluation – Term:

Physical &/or Sensory

Name of Intervention	Number of Learner Participants	Impact	Comments

SEND Intervention Annual Summary

Year: 2021–22

During the year a total of 138 interventions were provided to our learners with SEND. The distribution of interventions and perceived impact is summarised in the grid below. This information is collated during the year in consultation with staff facilitating the intervention and learners themselves.

Intervention Focus	Numbers Offered	Impact	Comments
Cognition & Learning	60	80% positive	Interventions generally well received by learners and staff. Where impact was not positive, additional assessment has been commissioned.
Communication & Interaction	45	85% positive	Various interventions were new this year and were popular with learners. Impact was high and agreed to continue to use where appropriate in future.
Social, Emotional & Mental Health	24	70% positive	Generally, interventions were positive but a new framework for understanding emotions was piloted. Less popular than previous approach so will be replaced next year.
Physical &/or Sensory	9	95% positive	Learners involved were highly motivated and activities were popular and enjoyable. Good results which have transferred into other activities. Programmes will remain.

SEND Intervention Annual Summary

Year:

During the year a total of ▌interventions were provided to our learners with SEND. The distribution of interventions and perceived impact is summarised in the grid below. This information is collated during the year in consultation with Staff facilitating the intervention and learners themselves.

Intervention Focus	Numbers Offered	Impact	Comments
Cognition & Learning			
Communication & Interaction			
Social, Emotional & Mental Health			
Physical &/or Sensory			

Assimilating your professional evaluation of SEND interventions into the SEN information report each term can help to increase the dynamism and relevance of your SEN information report. The SEND Code of Practice (2014, updated 2015) tells us that the SEN information report needs to be reviewed and updated annually, but we are also encouraged to update the report during the year to capture changes. What better way to demonstrate your ongoing professional evaluation than to publish your summary of impact of interventions? You may have noticed that the focus here is to encourage you to evaluate the impact of interventions and not SEND provision as a whole, including adjustments and support. This is because the impact of interventions may be easier to quantify on a termly basis than adjustments and support. Of course, you will still account for the impact of teacher adjustments and support but your methods may be qualitative rather than the more quantitative evaluation used for interventions. For example, to evaluate the impact of teacher adjustments, you may plan to complete learning support walks at different times in the year, where you will observe evidence of adjustments implemented compared to those indicated in an adjustment menu. Similarly, you may complete sample observations that focus on the deployment of TAs and use of resources in classes to help quality assure practice and inform your professional evaluation of the effectiveness of resources. The richness of this data will help you to demonstrate the overall effectiveness of your SEND provision over time.

Learning Support Walk – Evidence of Adjustments

Completed by:

Date:

Class Visited:

Staff Present:

Context:

Anticipated Teacher Adjustments (highlight what is observed)

Cognition & Learning	Communication & Interaction	Social, Emotional & Mental Health	Physical &/or Sensory
• Teacher refers to alternative means of recording (voice recorder, type, film) • Sufficient time for task • Short 'bursts' of work • Step by step instructions • Visual prompts (YouTube clip, model example, photos or picture cards) • Pause to ask questions • Structured choices • Now & next structure	• Use concise language and visual prompts or models • Summarise key points • Pre teach key words • Check out understanding by asking questions • Explicit beginning and ending of task within agreed time limit • Advanced warning of change • Explain purpose of task	• Agree start and finish time • Make explicit task relevance • Praise effort & engagement • Learner & adult identifies success each day. • Set own goal for the week • Ask questions to encourage self-reflection • Learner selects task order • Share 'I can' statements	• Adapt materials so more accessible • Scaffold tasks so skills broken into small steps • Adapt working position • Reduce environmental noise and sufficient light • Pre-prepare resources to support access • Promote regular movement and posture change

Observation Comments:

Strengths:

Areas for Development:

Evaluation Summary:

Action Required:

Learning Support Walk – Evidence of Resources and Support

Completed by:

Date:

Class Visited:

Staff Present:

Context:

Anticipated Resources and Support (highlight what is observed)

Cognition & Learning	Communication & Interaction	Social, Emotional & Mental Health	Physical & or Sensory
• Electronic tablet, voice recorder, camera, laptop • Cubes, counters, Numicon • Writing boards, pencil grips, triangular pens • Post-its, notebook, whiteboard, • Sentence starters, word sheets, phonic cards • Story books, TV programmes, websites • Rehearse vertical, horizontal & circular shapes	• Social stories • Social scenario discussion cards • Reading comprehension cards for discussion • Story books, film clips • Question sheets • Word lists • Socially Speaking activities and game • My turn, your turn games • Phone conversations	• Weekly 'story' board recording successes each day • Letter to my teacher/friend/ self identifying highlights from week and next steps. • Positive rewards programme, stickers, Lego pieces • Visual timetable/ now and next board	• Headphones or ear defenders • Weighted cushion or blanket • Inflatable ball, wedge cushion, • Wobble board • PE equipment, skipping rope, ball, bean bag • Accessible scissors, pencils, pens • Regular sensory walks

Observation Comments:

Strengths:

Areas for Development:

Evaluation Summary:

Action Required:

Learning Support Walk – Evidence of TA Deployment

Completed by:

Date:

Class Visited:

Staff Present:

Context:

Anticipated Deployment (highlight what is observed)

Mediation	Reinforcement
Assessment	Intervention

Observation Comments:

Strengths:

Areas for Development:

Evaluation Summary:

Action Required:

The focus of our next book in *The Essential SENCO Toolkit* series is upon SEND quality assurance: intent, implementation and impact, where we will explore aspects of monitoring, strategic planning and evaluation. In the meantime, ensure that the purpose of your actions is defined along with their *anticipated* impact. Also try to capture the *actual* implementation of interventions. There is a risk that after half a term, you may conclude that an intervention is not working for a learner, as it appears that they have made limited or no progress. Of course, this may be true, but it is also possible that you were not 'working the intervention'. For example, if the plan was for the learner to participate in an activity twice weekly for five weeks, but this was only delivered in the first and fourth week, due to staff absence, then it is unfair to attribute the limited progress to the intervention. As with all aspects of our role, we must gather information about the whole context in order to make an informed evaluation.

Implications for SENCOs and SEN Practitioners

Capturing the impact of SEND provision requires a clear and explicit understanding of the provision offer and its actual application. That is why it is essential that SENCOs and SEN Practitioners fulfil and/or delegate the monitoring and quality assurance aspect of their leadership role. Best practice is to ensure that all leaders in the school or setting are regularly monitoring the impact of SEND provision. To do this, they need to know *what* is offered, *why* this is offered (and not something else) and *how* they will know if it makes a difference. Adapting monitoring forms to include regular focused observations or learning walks that seek to gather evidence of the impact of a particular aspect of SEND provision, increases the likely occurrence of monitoring in these areas. Creating an annual schedule for such information gathering will help to protect the time necessary for engagement, whilst also raising the profile and importance of the activity and, by implication, the importance of the impact of SEND provision. As obvious as that may sound, it should not always be assumed that the expectation that SEND provision will have a positive impact on overcoming or removing barriers to learning, is a given. In reality, SEND provision itself is in danger of becoming a 'norm' or an expectation of sustainable need. The risk with this is that, because it is 'always' required, it may be assumed that its impact is limited and, by implication, less significant. Of course, nothing could be further from the truth! **Yes, SEND provision is an ongoing requirement but it should be as dynamic, personalised and varied as the learners that it is aimed at. If your SEND provision has become predictable and repetitive, immediately seek to evaluate its relevance to the learners it is aimed at!**

> **Reflections**
>
> - Is there a shared expectation that SEND provision will have a positive impact on learners or is it assumed that it is simply ongoing?
> - Who monitors the impact of SEND provision and how is this gathered?
> - Are you able to evidence-base that your described SEND provision actually happens?

References

Special Educational Needs and Disability Code of Practice: 0 to 25 years – Statutory Guidance for Organisations which Work with and Support Children and Young People who have Special Educational Needs or Disabilities (2014; updated 2015). Department for Education and Department of Health.

10. Getting started – the 7 Ps of SEND Provision

It appears that we are now embarking on the last chapter of this book! Which means it is that time where our focus moves towards *your* reflections and ideas for actions. I would like to thank you for investing time reading or scanning *SEND Intervention* and I hope it has inspired additional thinking around this essential topic. I also hope that you can now spend some time thinking about the implementation of your thinking and you can identify what you will do as a result of reading or scanning this book. What will be your starting point for action? At the end of *SEND Assessment* (book 1), you were encouraged to consider implementing the 7 Cs Learning Portfolio, as a language for SEND assessment. So, in the spirit of consistency, I want to now encourage you to consider the 7 Ps of SEND Provision.

The 7 Ps of SEND Provision, outlined below, are intended to provide a framework for your own analysis of the quality and diversity of your provision.

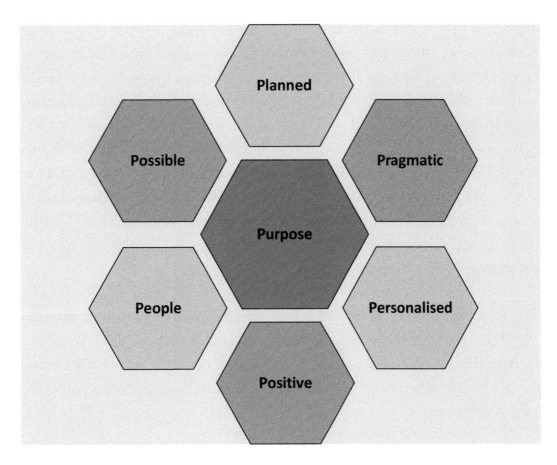

DOI: 10.4324/9781003179436-10

The 7 Ps of SEND Provision

1: Purpose

At the heart of effective SEND provision is clarity of purpose. That is why much of this text has recapped the language of assessment and revisited the very definition of SEND. Understanding *what* you are trying to achieve by providing something additional to or different from the curriculum offer available to others of the same age, is essential. **So often we connect learners to interventions or TAs, without thoughtfully 'anticipating' what we expect to be different as a result. By defining the anticipated impact of provision, it helps us to reflect on the 'actual' impact of provision over time. Without such clarity our focus is often on whether the learner engaged with the provision and enjoyed it.** Of course, engagement and enjoyment are important and highly relevant, especially for the learner, but for what purpose? *Why* do you want the learner to take part in an intervention? What skills do you hope to promote from this participation? How will it be useful to them? What will they gain from it? How will you know they have gained this? **The provision needs to be selected for its relevance to that individual learner and its potential to contribute to development.**

2: Plan

Effective SEND provision must be planned. Planning incorporates the thoughtful process of purpose, where you can reflect on the individual anticipated impact of the provision, but planning also ensures appropriate delivery. For teachers to make relevant adjustments or tweaks to enhance quality-first teaching, they must have knowledge of learner need and knowledge of adaptations. Planning staff development and promoting knowledge and skills is an essential part of the role of the SENCO and/or SEN Practitioner. Communicating the learning profile of a class to a supply teacher is vital, along with information about additional provision for learners with SEND or indeed other groups of learners. The SEND profile Venn diagram (Figure 2.1) presented in Chapter 2 can be useful for this, along with the practical strategy class list (Figure 7.7) from Chapter 7.

Planning access to support, be it additional adult support or resources, is essential, as is the need to plan *what* is done by the additional adult or how the resources will be applied. Interventions are also only possible with planning. This includes planning the time in the day when they will take place, who will attend, who will deliver and where they will meet.

3: Pragmatic

SEND provision with purpose must also be pragmatic. Ultimately the provision should lead to positive change that benefits the learner. They should, in time, be able to 'gain' something tangible from the provision, be it greater fluency and accuracy of a skill, independence with skill application, new knowledge and/or skills, that can be applied to other contexts (transcendence,) as well as confidence and a greater insight into how they learn, behave or communicate with others. The *Cambridge English Dictionary* defines pragmatic as "solving problems in a sensible way that suits the conditions that really exist now, rather than obeying fixed theories, ideas or rules". This definition appears to be particularly pertinent to planning SEND provision with purpose, both in terms of its emphasis on the conditions that really exist now and the desire to resolve problems in a sensible way. **It is essential that SEND provision is planned for the context in which it will be implemented.** For SENCOs and SEN Practitioners this is about the classroom or subject rooms where learners will be working. It must involve the learner themselves and the adults (TAs, parents or carers) that are working with them. **SEND provision cannot be an 'add-on' but must be a fully integrated part of the whole school and class provision.**

4: Personalised

Effective SEND provision is personalised to the assessed strengths and needs of each learner. Knowledge of learner strengths is particularly relevant, as they represent the foundations to build upon. In real terms, if a learner is identified as having social communication and friendship skills as a strength, then utilising peer supporters and promoting social learning and/or coaching could be really effective for them. If speech, language and listening skills are strengths, then conversational teaching and the use of questions could be useful. Similarly, if making things, gross and fine motor skills are strengths, then promoting learning opportunities which involve physical movement could also be effective. In the same way, if these are areas for development, this mode of delivery will be less effective. Planning SEND provision with purpose involves personalisation. **Learners should not be 'matched' to the interventions that are available in the school or setting, but rather, the interventions should be targeted to meet an identified purpose or address a particular barrier to learning. We cannot only offer what is in the 'cupboard' or what has historically always been on offer. Our SEND provision should be dynamic and responsive to each learner cohort.** Of course, availability of published interventions and resources is a significant issue and challenge for SENCOs and SEN Practitioners, particularly at a time of budget constraints. However, SEND provision is not always about buying the latest resource or approach; instead, it is about personalised and supportive teaching, which has direction and purpose. The issue of 'to buy or not to buy' resources and interventions was explored in Chapter 8, and suffice to say that, spending large amounts of money on an intervention, will not in itself generate personalisation or guarantee progress.

5: Positive

Effective SEND provision is positive, both in terms of its intention, delivery and experience. If the learner or the adult working with them (teacher, TA or parent/carer) does not have a positive approach or belief in the purpose of the provision (adjustment, support or intervention), then the provision will be less effective. Adults are crucial in setting the 'tone' and expectations linked to provision. If, for example, the teacher is reluctant to make adjustments, or adjustments are presented as an 'after-thought' then the potential impact of the adjustment is reduced. The learner may even lose confidence or feel apologetic, angry or perceive themselves as 'different' to others. Similarly, if resources and support are not integrated positively into the teaching and learning expectations of the class, then the same 'awkwardness' may emerge. For example, if a teacher responds to a learner's request to use an alternative means of recording with a comment such as "if you must", this utterly devalues both the learner and the resource. In the same way, if the teacher is not seen as the commissioner of an intervention, and they appear unaware that an individual or small group of learners have been asked to engage with an activity inside or outside of the classroom, the likelihood of generalisation of the intervention skills is diminished. **Adults and learners need to have a shared positive attitude towards engagement with SEND provision for it to have any meaning or purpose.**

6: Possible

Effective SEND provision must be possible. Teacher adjustments and tweaks need to be realistic and achievable. Support and resources need to be available as and when required and interventions need to be 'doable' alongside the curriculum offer. It is often this latter requirement that is the greatest challenge for SENCOs and SEN Practitioners. How to organise interventions that do not deny learners other learning opportunities? **Building 'self-directed' learning *into* the curriculum offer or weekly timetable makes interventions far more possible. For example, if every learner at some point in the day has 20 or 30 minutes to either individually pursue a skill or topic of interest, complete a targeted intervention, rehearse spoken language, play social games or activities, imagine how many 'add-ons' would become an integrated part of the school day?** This has the potential to benefit all learners, including those who are high-attaining and those who need time to consolidate their understanding or rehearse a skill. It can benefit those who need more opportunities to develop spoken English if it is their second language. It can provide 'space' for reflection and analysis and it can provide time to deliver relevant and purposeful SEND interventions. This time helps to make SEND provision possible.

7: People

Planning effective SEND provision with purpose requires active involvement of people. This includes the learner themselves, the teacher or teachers, TAs and of course, the parents and/or carers. Provision is not something that is 'done' *to* someone, but rather done *with* them. Teacher tweaks or adjustments should always be 'checked out' with the learner. For example, the teacher can ask the learner if it is easier if they summarise instructions with them at the end? Or is it useful to have instructions on blue paper? Learners should be encouraged to choose resources and/ or support that may help them. Adults should ask the learner whether it is useful to record their ideas using a 'talking tin' or read text with the electronic reading pen? The learner may need to try a variety of resources in order to gain the necessary experience to express a preference, but it is essential that they are involved in the process of selection. Similarly, seeking support from an adult: currently, we tend to deploy adults to work with learners, and it is the adults who determine the focus of the work or support provided. But just imagine, what impact could it have if a TA asked a learner "how can I best help you today?" The learner themselves would then be required to think about the support they need and to do this, they would need to understand what had been asked! This could be very different to the situation where the TA may end up getting the learner's pencil, opening their book and directing them to write the date on 'this' line. Of course, some of your learners may not yet be ready for this sort of questioning, but isn't this level of independence and empowerment what we are ultimately seeking for learners? Do we not want all learners to be engaged, reflective and independent? **The risk is that the very introduction of SEND provision can, for some learners, reduce their independence and even their efficacy and confidence as they perceive that they need 'help' with all tasks.**

To summarise, planning SEND provision with purpose involves a clear understanding of the anticipated impact of provision and a clear sense of purpose. The 7 Ps are intended to encourage your own reflection so that you can hold yourself to account when reviewing your SEND provision and implementing your annual provision mapping process. It is hoped that the simple questions in the provision wheel below will act as a practical reminder to help you.

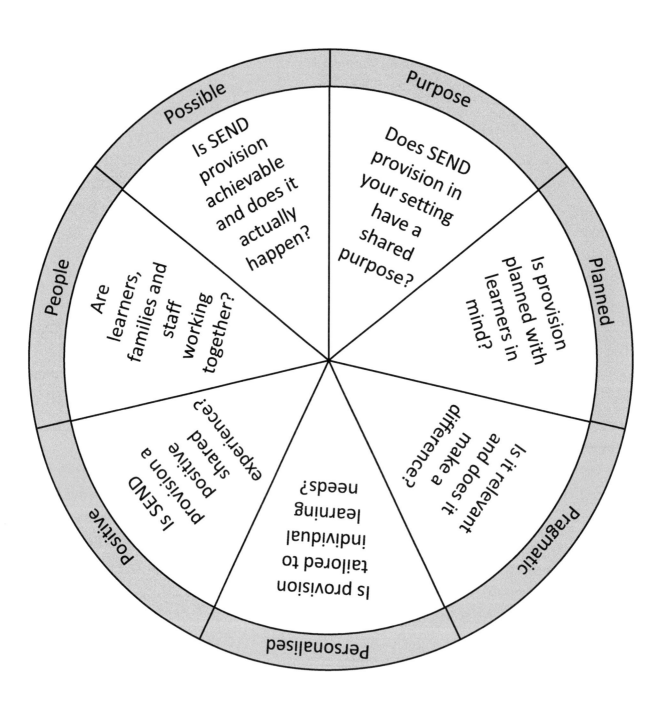

SEND Intervention – Professional's Action Planning Tool

What I liked about the book:

What resonated the most with me at this time was:

What I would like to do as a result of reading this book:

How could I achieve this?

What barriers may I face?

How can I 'overcome' or 'remove' these barriers?

Who would be interested in working with me on this?

What do I need to do first?

Implications for SENCOs and SEN Practitioners

The ultimate implication for SENCOs and SEN Practitioners is to ensure that your SEND Provision is planned with purpose. This can be achieved with an awareness of *what* **you do,** *why* **you do this instead of something else and** *how* **you know it makes a difference.** These three questions take us back to the start of the book, indicating the cyclical nature of this topic and our work. So, for now, it is also where we will stop. In our next book, we will combine all that we have discovered regarding SEND assessment and intervention, but this time through the lens of SEND monitoring and quality assurance. Until then, keep up the incredible work you do and continue to champion all of our learners, valuing their unique and individual contributions.

References

Cambridge English Dictionary (2020). 'Pragmatic'. Available at https://dictionary.cambridge.org/dictionary/english/pragmatic (Accessed 1 May 2021).

SEND Assessment: A Strengths-based Framework for Learners with SEND (2021) Judith Carter. Abingdon: Routledge Speechmark.

Index

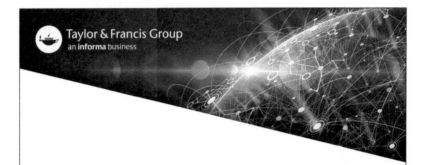